PAST and PRESENT

No 61

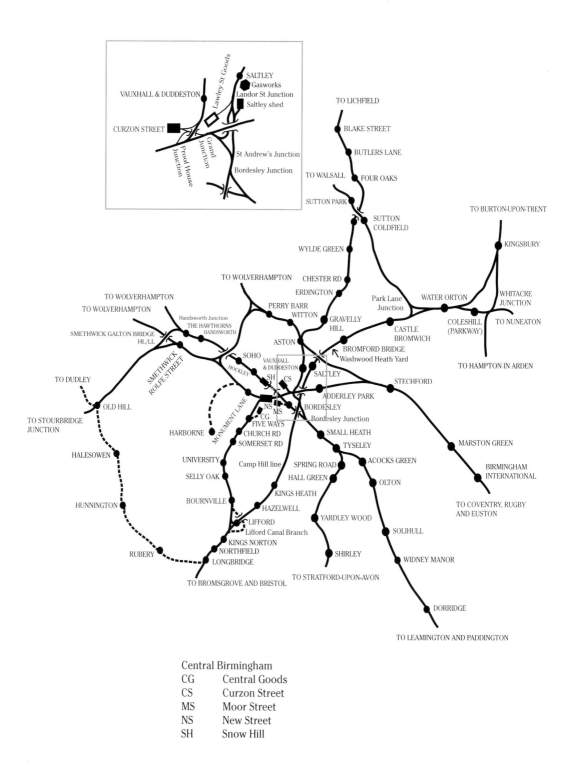

Central Birmingham
CG   Central Goods
CS   Curzon Street
MS   Moor Street
NS   New Street
SH   Snow Hill

Map of the area covered by this book, showing locations featured or referred to in the text.

BRITISH RAILWAYS

PAST and PRESENT

No 61

Birmingham

Geoff Dowling and John Whitehouse

Past and
Present

Past & Present Publishing Ltd

To Irene and Daphne
Thank you for your support and patience!

First published in 2010

British Library Cataloguing in Publication Data

A catalogue record for this book is available from the
British Library.

ISBN 978 1 85895 260 4

Past & Present Publishing Ltd
The Trundle
Ringstead Road
Great Addington
Kettering
Northants NN14 4BW

Tel/Fax: 01536 330588
email: sales@nostalgiacollection.com
Website: www.nostalgiacollection.com

Printed and bound in the Czech Republic

ACKNOWLEDGEMENTS

Particular thanks are due to Michael Mensing, David C. Williams, Roger Shenton, John
Dew and Paul Dorney for providing photographs for use in this volume, and Michael Den-
holm, Mick Naughton, Richard Tuplin and John Wright for their help in providing invalu-
able information to ensure that the text is as accurate as possible.

**UNIVERSITY: This view of the Birmingham West Suburban Railway looking south from the overbridge at
University station reveals a sharp curve as the railway follows the contour of the Birmingham & Worcester
Canal south to Selly Oak. The fencing at this point is looking a bit rickety to the point of being non-existent,
a far cry from the forest of palisade fencing that fringes the railway today. On 15 March 1962 BR Standard
Class 5 No 73028 heads a northbound working, probably a Gloucester to Birmingham train judging by the
coaching stock.**

**The palisade fencing is now firmly in situ, albeit mercifully hidden behind the self-setting trees that
have appeared in recent years. The buildings on the right belong to the Queen Elizabeth Hospital, and in
recent years the site has been developed further as evidenced by the dominant chimney stack. The electrification masts also add an extra dimension as a pair of Class 323 units, with No 323242 leading, slow for the
station forming the 12.23 Longbridge to Four Oaks service on 5 March 2009.** *Peter Shoesmith/GD*

Contents

CURZON STREET was Birmingham's first station, opening in 1838. It was a terminus station serving both the London & Birmingham Railway and the Grand Junction Railway, but was used as such only until 1854, when the more centrally located New Street opened. Thereafter it served as a goods station until 1966, when for a period of years it was neglected, and even threatened with demolition. The building, which is in the Roman style, was designed by Philip Hardwick (who also designed Euston station) and complemented the famous (but now demolished) Doric Arch at Euston. It survives as one of the most significant pieces of railway architecture in the world, and is now owned by the City Council, which has secured its future. *GD*

Introduction

There is probably no better place to reflect the varying fortunes of Britain's railway system than the City of Birmingham, as it has stood at the core of the network since the first fledgling lines radiating from London and Liverpool converged at the new Curzon Street terminus in 1838. Since then Birmingham has remained at the crossroads. Whether your travel plans involve venturing from Edinburgh and Newcastle to Bristol and the South West, or Glasgow and Carlisle to Reading and the South East, New Street will be on your route.

In the great railway age of the second half of the 19th century Birmingham came to be served by three of the biggest companies, the London & North Western, the Midland and the Great Western, which reflected the growing importance of the city as a centre for both commerce and industry. This prosperity flowed over into the 20th century and was reflected in the provision of the two great stations of New Street and Snow Hill. The cities stature continued to grow to the point where it is now England's 'second city' after London in terms of population.

Birmingham's development was based on the Industrial Revolution, which began a few miles away at Coalbrookdale in the Severn Gorge, and it became known as either 'the workshop of the world' or 'the city of a thousand trades', both reflecting the skills and versatility that developed in the area. It also became the financial centre of the region, whose influence spread far beyond the city boundary. The Midland Bank, for instance, once the biggest in the UK and now part of the HSBC Group, was formed in the city and had its original head office next to New Street station.

However, it is the motor trade that became synonymous with the name Birmingham, as throughout the first half of the 20th century vehicle production flourished, led by the Austin Motor Company, which established its base at Longbridge on the southern boundary of Greater Birmingham. And it was the motor car, and road transport in general, that spelled the end of the first railway age, offering more versatility than trains.

By the early 1960s road transport was considered the future. Increased personal prosperity, cheap cars and an improving road network saw the closure of many railways; this was to have a significant impact on Birmingham, which by this time had embraced the title of 'Motor City'. Due to its central geographic location, it was also at the hub of the road network, while the role of the railway was becoming significantly downgraded and its role revised, with a strategy of concentrating on long-distance journeys, where it retained an advantage. It was this strategy change that brought about the West Coast Electrification Scheme, which included the main line from Euston to Liverpool and Manchester as well as the routes via Birmingham and the West Midlands.

Electrification brought considerable benefits to Birmingham, but there was a down side: the Great Western lines were either closed or downgraded, including a move that would have been unthinkable a few years earlier, the complete closure of Snow Hill. The complex at New Street was rebuilt, and it perhaps speaks volumes that no extractor fans were included in the scheme as it was anticipated that the majority of trains would be electrically hauled! But the railway refused to lie down and die. There was a significant residual demand for rail travel, particularly from local commuters; these were becoming increasingly active, as British Rail found to its cost every time it tried to close the North Warwickshire Line. By the early 1970s the road network was beginning to suffer from congestion and the move back to rail was under way.

During the 1970s control of the local transport network, including trains, in an area stretching from Wolverhampton to Coventry and including the Birmingham conurbation, came under the control of a local transport authority. The organisation had sufficient influence that the suggestion of expansion of local transport services became a reality, culminating in the creation of the Cross City line between Lichfield and Redditch in 1978, which included the provision of new stations. Electrification followed in 1993, and two years later the Jewellery Line opened, following the course of the old Great Western route north from a reopened Snow Hill. Snow Hill Tunnel also reopened as part of the scheme, which meant that South Midlands services could again access Snow Hill, and a second Cross City route was formed, from Dorridge to Stourbridge. The foresight of local councils to protect the old Great Western route was further justified by the opening of the Midland Metro tram system in 1997.

Privatisation of the railways, which took place during this period of growth, also played its part, particularly with Chiltern Railways and Virgin Trains, which brought significant service improvements. Chiltern, which operates services out of London Marylebone and has re-energised the old Great Western route to Birmingham, has also been responsible for a good part of the improvements to Birmingham Moor Street, while Virgin now runs three trains per hour each weekday between New Street and Euston. It is difficult to imagine this sort of investment having taken place under state control.

Future plans include extending the Midland Metro system into the city centre, with street running, and a £600m scheme to improve passenger facilities at New Street has just a commenced. The sadness is that opportunities have been missed to actually improve the train-handling capacity of the station by providing new platforms, a decision that will severely affect its future ability to accommodate further service growth. However, there is talk of a new high-speed line encompassing Birmingham, an exciting prospect for the future, and one that may also be New Street's salvation.

Uncared for and unloved maybe, dear old New Street still manages to meet the demands of the railway and more than 120,000 passengers each day, which is a remarkable feat as it was only designed to accommodate half that number. The new plans are mainly focussed on the passenger concourse, which will be greatly expanded and, from artist's impressions, should fit in well with the surrounding modernistic architecture of the Bull Ring. With 'High Speed 2' perhaps getting ever closer, maybe this is Birmingham's second railway age!

This volume, which is not intended to be a definitive railway history of Birmingham, is the first of two, with the second covering the surrounding area to the north consisting of South and East Staffordshire. The majority of our 'past' scenes relate to the period from 1955 through to the end of steam, and provide an illustration of how Birmingham's railway network has changed – whether for better or worse is for you, the reader, to decide.

The compilation of this volume, as with the others, has been exciting, informative, revealing, frustrating and inspirational, with perhaps a few more emotions best glossed over. This is mainly due to the fact that when trying to cover a location there is often no way of knowing what to expect. In the introduction to Volume 5 of this series we commented on the difficulty posed by trees and the like. Now, more than 20 years later, those trees have become mini-forests, and Network Rail has erected what many believe to be awful palisade fencing in the name of health and safety. Getting the 'present' photograph is just half the task; the second bit is writing about it, and as always there have been many 'eureka' moments, or murmurs of 'Well! I didn't know that!' It only serves to underline that there is always something new to learn, even if it is just a new architectural term!

Throughout this volume the name Peter Shoesmith crops up many times. Peter was a prolific photographer throughout his life, and not just of railways. He was different from many photographers who covered the last 15 years of steam in that he recorded all of the scene and not just the train. He was not a 'name', but his work demands wider coverage due to its sheer quality. Sadly, he died in 1995 before his work could be fully appreciated. Hopefully this volume will go a small way in redressing that omission.

While we have always attempted to get as close as possible to the footprints of the original photographer, it has not always been possible. But where we have failed, for whatever reason, this is explained in the text.

May your journey around the Birmingham of yesterday and today provide you with the same enjoyment and interest that it has given the authors.

Geoff Dowling   John Whitehouse

Birmingham New Street

BIRMINGHAM NEW STREET: The inadequacy of Curzon Street, Birmingham's first station, to meet the growing demands for rail travel led to the decision to build a new, grand, centrally located station that would match the aspirations of the city as it continued to expand as a major centre of commerce and industry. When the first trains used the still incomplete station in 1852 it was referred to as 'Grand Central Station', before the name of 'New Street' was finally adopted later that year. This is the scene looking west along the then Platform 3 (later Platform 6) in the mid-1930s, showing clearly the footbridge that spanned the station and was designated a public footpath, thus requiring that it should be an 'open station'. Ticketing stops were therefore necessary at fringe stations for revenue protection. Queens Drive, which ran through the centre of the station, is to the left and Navigation Street road bridge can be seen in the distance.

The equivalent platform today is No 6, looking from the 'A' end again towards Navigation Street, the bridge abutment being visible in the background between the two platform ends. This view emphasises the gloom due to the virtual absence of light over the running lines. The station is classified as an underground station following the disastrous 1987 King's Cross tube station fire. Note, too, the relatively narrow platforms for such a busy station. Miss P, Nicklin, *GD collection/GD*

BIRMINGHAM NEW STREET: The crowning glory of the new station was a mammoth 212-foot trussed-arch single-span roof, designed by E. A. Cowper of the firm Fox, Henderson & Co of Smethwick, who had also been responsible for the roof at Paddington station and the Crystal Palace. This view, also from Platform 3 (later Platform 6) but looking east, gives an indication of the scale of the roof, which extended virtually the whole length of the station. The gabled buildings of Worcester Street can be seen in the distance, and New Street No 1 signal box is just visible as a train is seen working up the incline from Proof House Junction into the station. On the right is the entrance to the east-end subway, which ran beneath the station. The foreground trolleys give a graphic indication of the extent the railways were used for the carriage of goods in the mid-1930s, while the young enthusiast, maybe, has an interest in the locomotive, which appears to be standing on one of the middle roads between Platforms 1 and 2.

The approach to New Street from Proof House Junction has always been difficult, as the railway first goes into a dip immediately after the junction, then ascends a sharp incline through the tunnel to reach the summit virtually at the end of New Street's platforms. This is compounded by the severe curvature of the track into the body of the station, which means that even with modern stock drivers have to exercise great skill on the station approach. The sharpness of the curvature is well illustrated as Class 323 No 323241 cautiously departs from Platform 8a with the 1027 Redditch to Lichfield Trent Valley service. *Miss P. Nicklin, GD collection/GD*

BIRMINGHAM NEW STREET's reconstruction is well under way on 29 August 1964 as ex-LNER Class 'B1' No 61327 works into Platform 8 at the head of a summer Saturday working, the 0910 Weston-super-Mare to Sheffield Midland service. LNER traction was not common in New Street, being confined normally to 'B1s' working in on summer-dated workings. The train has just passed beneath the new Hill Street bridge, and the demolition of Queens Drive is in an advanced stage to the right of the locomotive. On the far right is the new parapet for the Navigation Street overbridge.

The platform number may have changed – this is now Platform 10 – but the position of both Hill Street and Navigation Street bridge parapets firmly places the location today. Between the two is the location of the entrance to Queens Drive. On 5 August 2009 Class 323 No 323204 departs with the 1218 Four Oaks to Redditch service. *David C. Williams/GD*

BIRMINGHAM NEW STREET: On 27 April 1963 the reconstruction of New Street has yet to begin, and in any event the prime consideration of the passengers of this Brockenhurst to New Street via Bournemouth and Bath football special will be the result of that afternoon's FA Cup semi-final between Southampton and Manchester United at nearby Villa Park. Bristol Barrow Road's 'Jubilee' No 45682 *Trafalgar* heads the rake of Southern green-liveried Mark I coaches into Platform 7. Behind the locomotive is Queens Drive, which effectively divided the station into two distinct segments, this being the Midland side with the old LNWR train shed on the other side. Oh, by the way, United won 1-0 and went on to win the FA Cup.

The scene changed very quickly, and by 25 July 1964 a hole is all that remains of Queens Drive as work on reconstruction is now well under way. In the 1885 extension project the station had been greatly enlarged with the provision of four new through platforms, covered by a graceful semi-circular roof. This was the new Midland side of the station, with Queens Drive providing the clear demarcation with their neighbour, the LNWR. However, as this scene reveals, work has commenced on dismantling the once graceful roof over the Midland platforms and a new temporary footbridge has been provided for the duration of the work. Note also how the connection from the through road only now connects with that off Platform 7, where BR Standard Class 4 No 76088 awaits the arrival of 'Black 5' No 45305 on an inter-regional express. No 45305 survived the cutter's torch and, as part of the '5305 Locomotive Society' fleet, is still active on the main line and heritage railways to this day.

The scene today has opened out considerably, and the skyline has benefited, with both new buildings and the external refurbishment of existing structures. On the extreme right is part of the staircase from the new Navigation Street access and footbridge that connects all platforms except 1 and 12. Interestingly, this was predicted in 1964 with the provision of the temporary footbridge in roughly the same location. Queens Drive's demise provided space in which to increase New Street's platform capacity, which means that it is not straightforward to compare like with like. Class 170 No 170517 is arriving at the present Platform 7 on 11 August 2009, with the parapet of Navigation Street to the right and the location of the entrance to Queens Drive above the DMU. Class 221 Cross-Country 'Voyager' No 221123 awaits its next turn in the centre road between Platforms 7 and 8. The background Class 350 EMU occupies the new bay Platform 4C, which was provided recently in a desperate attempt to increase capacity and operating flexibility. *David C. Williams/ Peter Shoesmith/GD*

BIRMINGHAM NEW STREET: The Parcels Bay and Fish Bay were tucked away on the south side of the station abutting Hill Street, with a public entrance from Station Street. On the extreme right is the facade of the Futurist cinema, so long a Birmingham landmark, which was the first to show 'talkies' in the city during March 1929. Birmingham has long boasted one of the best fresh-fish markets in the country, yet being probably one of the furthest from the sea. The answer is, of course, that the market enjoyed excellent rail connections to the key fishing ports as well as the dedicated facility at New Street station. In June 1959 Stanier 'Black 5' No 45272 stands at the head of a working from the fish dock.

Look closely at the top right-hand corner of the 'present' view, and the corner of the old Futurist cinema is visible. It ceased to be a cinema some years ago, and is now a nightclub. The concrete ramp climbing off Hill Street provides access to the upper car park; this was built on top of the original station car park, which sits on the concrete slab that now spans the station. Class 323 No 323218 prepares to leave from Platform 11 with the 1214 service from Lichfield City to Longbridge. A bay platform can be seen in the background, which in the past was used by mail trains until the business was lost to road. The west-end subway, one of two constructed in the 1885 expansion, was extended into the nearby Post Office sorting office, thus providing ready access to the station for the mail. *Peter Shoesmith/GD*

BIRMINGHAM NEW STREET is seen here at the extreme west end looking back into the 'rectangle' formed by Hill Street (from where this photograph was taken) and Navigation, Summer and Swallow Streets. The date is 15 April 1961 and 'Jubilee' No 45685 Barfleur, departing with the 1248 York to Bristol Temple Meads service, is about to negotiate the severe curvature and gradient of the West Midland Suburban route as it enters into the series of tunnels through to Five Ways. Note that the turntable, which had been positioned beneath the retaining wall of Navigation Street, has been dismantled and only the pit and radiating roads remain. Enhancing the background is the attractive frontage of the Birmingham Garages building, complete with an example of 1950s-style Esso logo and petrol pumps. The distinctive upper body of a Birmingham Corporation omnibus completes the scene.

The old turntable site is now occupied by Birmingham New Street signal box, which, no doubt to the joy of Network Rail, is a Grade 2 listed building of the British school of architecture. Completed in 1964 , the four-storey building dominates the locality as well as controlling movements within New Street and its environs. Saltley and Gloucester are its fringe boxes. Note the 'Mailbox' behind the signal box, which was once a huge Royal Mail sorting office but is now an up-market shopping mall and apartment block. The complexity of the layout here is mirrored by the overhead electric wiring; in addition to the Euston to Wolverhampton route, Lichfield Trent Valley to Redditch is also now fully electrified. *Michael Mensing/GD*

BIRMINGHAM NEW STREET: A murky New Year's Eve in 1965 reveals New Street to be little more than a building site masquerading as a station. However, look closely and the framework of the 'new' station is beginning to take shape. This is the scene looking back into Platforms 7 and 8 (under the current numbering plan) as BR Standard Class 4 No 76058 eases away from the latter with what looks like a relatively light load. The concrete beam will eventually carry the pavement and road that forms the main entrance to New Street off Smallbrook Queensway, a new dual carriageway and thoroughfare that replaced Worcester Street. Note the piece of angle-iron bolted to the concrete beam above the loco – it has relevance.

The finished product! That piece of angle-iron was there for a purpose, which was to support an overhead electrification structure! The beam has been discoloured over the years by diesel exhaust fumes, while beyond the parapet of the bridge is a glimpse of the facade of the station. Platform 6, which in 1965 looked a grim place to await a train, is occupied by a Virgin 'Pendolino' on a Euston diagram, while from Platform 8 Class 323242 emerges with the 1523 Longbridge to Four Oaks service. *Peter Shoesmith/GD*

16

BIRMINGHAM NEW STREET: At the eastern end on 25 March 1963 an unidentified 'Jubilee' awaits departure from Platform 7 with an inter-regional express. It is on the 'Midland' side of the station and is under the control of New Street No 2 signal box, which can be seen on the right. The 'Jubilee' is drawn up so that its chimney is just under the girder bridge that carries Queens Drive into the centre of the station, behind which can be seen the distinctive gabled buildings that front onto Worcester Street. A DMU, representing the new order, stands at Platform 8, and will be engaged on a local working. Meanwhile, the 'Jubilee' seems to be under intense scrutiny from the man in front of the signal box – a penny for his thoughts? The reconstruction of New Street coincided with the rebuilding of much of the east side of Birmingham city centre, especially around the Bull Ring area. A consequence of this was that the gabled buildings, for so long a feature of the area, were demolished and replaced by a new road layout, Smallbrook Queensway, which considerably opened up the area and for once made it possible to look directly into the station. The 1960s regeneration has since been superseded by the 21st-century version as the new city skyline forms an impressive backdrop to Class 323220 arriving at Platform 11 with the 1440 Lichfield City to Longbridge service. Not all the buildings are new, as the Rotunda, the base of which can be seen centre left, is of 1960s vintage.
Peter Shoesmith/GD

BIRMINGHAM NEW STREET: Tucked away in the corner bordered by Station Street and Queens Drive was the imposing Midland Railway parcels office, which dated back to around the time of the enlargement of the station in 1885. It was connected to the main body of the station by an extension off the subway, constructed as part of the 1885 extension, which traversed the station, providing ready access to all platforms. Coincidentally, on 4 April 1957 an ex-Midland Railway Class 2P 4-4-0, No 40332, is waiting at the rear of a Redditch train at Platform 10, waiting to take over a later Bristol working. Note the fireman, who is busy shovelling coal forward in readiness for the next working.

The main entrance to the station off Smallbrook Ringway was built over the site of the parcels office, which was demolished as part of the reconstruction of the station. The date it ceased to be a parcels office is unclear, but in latter years it was used for sorting internal mail as well as becoming an administrative office for the railway. Beyond the glass screen is an area once occupied by British Rail's 'Red Star' parcels service. The bridge parapets indicate the respective access (right) and exit (left) lanes for vehicles. Class 220 'Voyager' No 220029 is arriving with the 1222 Newcastle-upon-Tyne to Reading cross-country service on 12 August 2009. *Michael Mensing/GD*

BIRMINGHAM NEW STREET was always popular with enthusiasts due to the variety of motive power to be seen, but they had to wait until the early 1960s for Stanier's 'Duchesses' to appear. This was simply due to the locomotives being too big for the limited clearances through the access tunnels. Pre-electrification work eased the clearance restrictions and from 1963 onwards they became regular performers on Euston trains. On 27 April No 46239 City of Chester restarts the 0940 Wolverhampton High Level to Euston service and is just about to enter the gloom of Worcester Street Tunnel. On the right is New Street No 1 signal box, which covered the eastern end of the old LNWR side of the station.

Without doubt Birmingham cannot be accused of being a city that stands still, and its civic motto 'Forward' is probably more apt than many realise. There can be no better illustration than the bold step to tear down the 1960s Bull Ring redevelopment, which so typified Birmingham as the 'Motor City', and replace it with a completely new pedestrian-orientated shopping centre, which now ranks as one of the best in the country (according to local publicity). The new skyline is very evident as Class 90 No 90019 (carrying First ScotRail livery, as it is nominally one of the locomotives used on the Caledonian sleeper services) eases into New Street with Virgin's 1143 service from London Euston on 1 May 2009. *David C. Williams/JW*

BIRMINGHAM NEW STREET: This is the view looking down into the old LNWR side of New Street in 1964. Once covered by the magnificent overall roof, years of neglect and wartime bomb damage caused the roof to be declared as dangerous, resulting in its removal in the immediate post-war years. Utilitarian canopies were provided as a replacement, which did not exactly enhance the place. Queens Hotel, on the right, for so long a dominant feature of this part of the city, closed and was demolished later in 1964. On the left, shuttering identifies the position of a new platform, while the debris indicates the removal of Queens Drive. No 1 signal box survives, but the new power box was already under construction and due for completion later that year, becoming operational during 1966.

The new station, which was completed in 1967 to coincide with the West Coast Electrification Scheme, was located beneath a concrete raft on top of which a shopping centre and two car parks were built. Consequently it became both gloomy and claustrophobic and quickly gained a poor reputation. It was designed for the age of the motor car when it was anticipated that demand for rail travel would decline. Predictably, usage has risen year on year and the demands placed upon New Street are now far beyond its design capability. Currently it sees more than 120,000 passengers per day, twice the projected throughput. The fact that it copes is to the credit of the people who run the station and the durability of the place. A $600m scheme to improve passenger facilities commenced in September 2009, but unfortunately there are no plans to increase platform capacity. On 5 August 2009 the 1230 service to London Euston departs with a Driving Van Trailer leading and a Class 90 electric locomotive propelling from the rear. The area will change considerably as part of the revamp. *David C. Williams/GD*

New Street to Smethwick Galton Bridge

ST VINCENT STREET (MONUMENT LANE): Class 25 No 25277 staggers out of Birmingham New Street's North Tunnel with a heavily laden car train from Longbridge on 28 March 1978. This was an unusual working as it was one of the few freights booked through New Street station at the time. The general scene of dereliction also perhaps represents the state of the city back in 1978, with the scrapyard and older background factories contrasting with the high-rise flats on the left and city landmark Alpha Tower on the right. Monument Lane engine shed was once situated on the right-hand side, while on the left was a fan of sidings.

The view from the very same St Vincent Street bridge today could not be more different, as the nose of an unidentified Class 170 emerges from beneath the concrete raft that now carries Birmingham's National Indoor Arena. The whole area was redeveloped in the late 1980s, with the NIA site merging into other developments, most notably the adjacent Brindley Place, to completely rejuvenate this area of the city. The NIA has a capacity of 13,000, which made it the largest in the UK when it opened in 1991, and is used primarily for major sporting events and concerts. Plans have been simmering for some time to open a station at this site to cater for the venue, but presently these are on the back burner! *Both GD*

MONUMENT LANE: This view looking back towards Monument Lane shed and the city centre presents a busy and contrasting vista of the changing face of Birmingham. The back-to-back houses on the left contrast with the new high-rise tower block, the latter to become a feature of the city. This undated early-1960s view also shows the onset of electrification, both with the erection of the overhead masts and also the demise of semaphore signalling. Monument Lane Goods Depot, in the background right, remains active with a Type 4 (later Class 40) diesel present on a rake of mineral wagons. A Class 08 is also engaged in shunting on the right, while in the centre background a Metro-Cammell Class 101 DMU is stabled awaiting its next turn. The main activity is Sulzer Type 2 diesel (later BR Class 24) No D5008 easing out of the yard with a rake of coaching stock. Pre-electrification, Type 2s were common on passenger turns in the area.

Looking at the same view today from Ladybrook Middleway presents a total contrast. The terraced houses have long since been demolished and the area is now parkland, while the land to the right has been redeveloped, but the avenue of trees presents a much more pleasant scene. Note how the city skyline has blossomed too, with a number of tower blocks now to be seen as well as the bulk of the National Indoor Arena, which covers the site of Monument Lane engine shed at the mouth of New Street's North Tunnel. Heading north on 3 April 2009 is an unidentified Virgin 'Voyager'. *Peter Shoesmith/GD*

MONUMENT LANE: A three-car Birmingham Railway Carriage & Wagon Co Class 104 DMU approaches the now closed Monument Lane station with a New Street-bound service. The station closed in 1958, but was still used as a 'ticketing stop' after closure as New Street was an open station. On the right is the six-road carriage shed, which by this time was being used to stable the DMUs that monopolised local services. At this point there were quadruple running lines; up and down goods lines ran from Monument Lane Goods Depot to Harborne Junction, the signals for which can be seen in the distance, while the up and down fast lines ran on each side of the island platform.

An unidentified Arriva Class 220 'Voyager' speeds past the site of Monument Lane station on 3 April 2009 with the 1327 Manchester Piccadilly to Bristol Temple Meads service. The track layout has changed, with only a double-track formation now in place, while the line on the extreme left is a long loop that runs down to St Vincent Street and is used mainly for empty stock workings awaiting access to New Street. *Peter Shoesmith/GD*

HARBORNE JUNCTION: The Harborne branch diverged from the Stour Valley route at a point roughly halfway between Monument Lane and the Dudley Road, and was accessed by a quite steeply inclined single-line spur that crossed the Wolverhampton Canal on a short girder bridge. The original plan was to connect Soho, on the nearby Great Western main line, to Lapal on the proposed Halesowen to Bromsgrove line. However, landowners objected and in the end only the 2½ miles from Harborne Junction to Harborne was ever built. Intermediate stations were located at Icknield Port Road, Rotton Park Road and Hagley Road. Initially it was very busy, but the growing popularity of buses and pathing problems into New Street led to the passenger service being withdrawn in 1934. The line remained open for freight until 1963, and just prior to final closure a three-car Derby-built Class 116 DMU eases from the junction with a Birmingham University Railways & Inland Waterways Society special on 17 March 1962.

The location today can be clearly identified as the abutments of the bridge that carried the branch over the canal remain in situ, the middle one no doubt a hazard to navigation due to its position in the waterway. On the main line a London Midland Class 153/170 combination working a Rugeley to Birmingham New Street service speeds past the site of the junction. It is good to note that many of the factories alongside the railway have survived into the 21st century. *Peter Shoesmith/GD*

HARBORNE JUNCTION: The bridge carrying the Harborne branch over the Wolverhampton Canal was a sturdy affair, no doubt because of both the tight curvature of the line and the gradient. The massive central abutment, positioned in the middle of the canal, is perhaps the most striking feature. A split-headcode Class 40 has just passed beneath the Dudley Road bridge on the approach to Harborne Junction at the head of a southbound express, most probably in the early 1960s before resignalling and pre-electrification work commenced around 1963.

Except for the bridge decking and the sprouting of several trees, the location today has not changed greatly. The bridge abutments remain, as does the impressive school building backing onto the railway. In a city that has seen so much change, this immediate area has perhaps seen least of all. On 3 April 2009 London Midland Class 323 No 323211 heads for Wolverhampton on a local stopping service. *Peter Shoesmith/GD*

HARBORNE BRANCH: The Birmingham University Railways & Inland Waterways Society special of 17 March 1962, seen earlier at Harborne Junction, is now pictured climbing towards Harborne, near Woodbourne Road, and overlooking the rural outlook of Chad Valley. This special train toured the Birmingham area, taking in more than 60 miles of track, including the Lifford Goods or Canal Branch (see page 66), all for the princely sum of 16 shillings, around 78p today.

The location today provides a fine walking route through to Harborne. The surrounding area has seen much development, so it is good to report that the public footpath that follows much of the old trackbed of the branch continues to give pleasure to the many seeking refuge from the pressures of city life. *Peter Shoesmith/GD*

HARBORNE: The end of the line, perhaps in more ways than one. D2387 shunts the yard at Harborne while undertaking the daily trip working on the branch. On the left coal is being unloaded into a Cooperative Society lorry from the rake of mineral wagons, while swarf metal shavings are deposited in both the lone central wagon and that on the right. The goods shed is on the left, while the remains of the station canopy and platform can be seen on the extreme right-hand side. Chad Valley Toys and Mitchells & Butlers were the two main organisations that kept the branch open until 1963. This scene is taken from the station footbridge.

After a period of dereliction following closure the site has now been redeveloped for residential purposes, and Frensham Way now occupies the site of the old goods yard. *Peter Shoesmith/GD*

SMETHWICK ROLFE STREET: A Metropolitan Cammell Class 101 DMU draws away from Smethwick Rolfe Street on 18 September 1964 with a Birmingham New Street to Wolverhampton High Level service. The station dates back to 1852 and has seen continuous service since. The footbridge crosses the railway on a diagonal as it follows the line of the road from which the station derives its name. The corner of the booking hall, which also faces out onto Rolfe Street, can be seen on the extreme left of the picture.

Rationalisation has reduced Rolfe Street to a shadow of its former self, with the footbridge, up-side buildings and canopy all being swept away with electrification. On the down platform the waiting room and canopy have also been demolished and a basic bus shelter is the only protection against the elements. However, note the top left-hand corner as the familiar outline of the booking hall remains, the one remaining link to the past. This is now the first station from New Street on the Stour Valley route and is served by the half-hourly all-stations service between New Street and Wolverhampton. On 5 August 2009 Class 323 No 323222 departs with the 1539 service from New Street.

Peter Shoesmith/JW

SMETHWICK GALTON BRIDGE (LOW LEVEL): A Class 104 scurries along the Stour Valley route on 22 October 1966 at the site now occupied by Galton Bridge station. Two bridges feature: the first carries the 'Stourbridge Extension' line from Smethwick Junction towards The Hawthorns, and behind that is the magnificent single-span structure over both the Stour Valley line and the parallel Birmingham Canal, which, when constructed by Thomas Telford in 1829, was the highest single-span bridge in the world, at 151 feet. It has Grade 1 listing status, and is now used by pedestrians only.

The location of the original photograph corresponds roughly with the booking hall at the new Galton Bridge station, which opened in 1995, together with the Jewellery Line that reconnected Snow Hill with the route to Stourbridge. Consequently, the view from the low-level down platform is the closest point to the 1966 scene nowadays, and shows the striking design of the station, which is similar to the other two new stations at The Hawthorns and Jewellery Quarter. The low-level route differs from the Jewellery Line as it is electrified, and recently introduced 'Desiro' Class 350 EMU No 350267 pauses with the 1434 Liverpool Lime Street to Birmingham New Street semi-fast service on 5 August 2009. *Michael Mensing/JW*

SMETHWICK GALTON BRIDGE (LOW LEVEL): This is the view from roughly the location of the booking hall at Galton Bridge looking along the Stour Valley towards Wolverhampton, with the Birmingham Canal just visible to the right of the locomotive. On 22 October 1966 the electrification work looks to be complete as English Electric Type 4 No D308 heads east with a rake of Gulf Oil four-wheel tanks, probably from the nearby Albion Oil Terminal.

The 'present' view is taken from Telford's bridge looking back towards the station, as Arriva Trains Wales Class 158 No 158840 restarts the combined 1138 Pwllheli and 1330 Aberystwyth service to Birmingham International on 5 August 2009. Look to the left of the apex of the station's middle lift shaft and there is just a glimpse of one of West Bromwich's tower blocks, which dominate the 1966 scene. The Stourbridge line platforms can also be glimpsed on the right. *Michael Mensing/JW*

30

New Street to Kings Norton, Longbridge and Halesowen

The route from Birmingham New Street to Kings Norton is now familiar to thousands of travellers each day, whether commuting into the city centre or travelling further afield to the South West. It was not always the case, as the original main line to the South West was via St Andrews Junction and the Camp Hill line, with a stub running from Kings Norton to a terminus at Granville Street, a short distance from New Street – this was the Birmingham West Suburban Railway, which opened in 1876. The connection to New Street was made in 1885, with the new line following a fresh alignment as far as Church Road, where a junction was made to provide a spur into a new goods yard, which became known as Birmingham Central Goods Depot.

ROLL UP, ROLL UP: Back in 1967 the railways were expected to carry virtually anything that was asked of them! There were specialist items of rolling stock for the majority of needs. Here the Crewe based Elephant Van M 37706 M is seen with a 'passenger' about to disembark - sadly his or her name was not recorded. *Ray Ruffell / Silver Link Archive*

BIRMINGHAM CENTRAL GOODS DEPOT (SUFFOLK STREET): What eventually became Birmingham Central Goods Depot began life as Worcester Wharf in 1887, which was an exchange facility between the Midland Railway and the Birmingham & Worcester Canal. The location was well chosen, as in time its position just off the city centre served it well. The terminus yard abutted Suffolk Street, which provided excellent vehicular access, although its existence was probably unknown to many as it was hidden behind hoardings that lined one side of the street. Railway access was by a branch from Church Road Junction, which ran at the rear on a slight embankment past Five Ways station before following its own alignment and through separate tunnels to the neighbouring Birmingham West Suburban Railway. This picture shows the scene around 1965, the year the landmark Rotunda building (far right) was opened. Centre left stands the Matthew Boulton Technical College, whose days were numbered as a place of teaching; it would soon be swallowed by the inner city redevelopment that took place in Birmingham in the late 1960s. How it contrasts with the then 'modern' architecture! The growth of road transport, especially as a consequence of the vastly improved links locally and Birmingham's close proximity to the growing motorway network, was rendering wagon-load rail freight uncompetitive, and facilities such as Central Goods were now on borrowed time, which finally ran out in 1967 when it closed. Demolition was not completed until 1973, when the aptly named Stanier House was built for British Rail. Indeed, the building boasted one of the nameplates of the 'Princess Coronation' Class locomotive No 46256 Sir William A. Stanier FRS, which was fixed to a wall in the reception area.

From the 1970s until more recent times most of the area once occupied by the goods yard was used for off-city-centre car-parking, but with the growth of land values it became a sought-after plot and is now the location of a number of modern office blocks. British Rail sold Stanier House, thus severing the last railway connection with the location, which has now been renamed Axis House; in view of the troubles between 1939 and 1945 this is not the brightest name, perhaps, especially as the goods yard was bombed during that period. *Peter Shoesmith/GD*

33

FIVE WAYS, the first station from New Street, opened in 1885 when the new connection was brought into use and is at the end of the series of tunnels that provide access to New Street station. The original station had rudimentary platform accommodation, and the building on the top left of this May 1968 view has been at various times a chapel and station booking hall, and survives today as commercial premises. The original station at Five Ways was temporarily closed in 1944, and this became permanent in 1950. The exit from New Street was both curvaceous and against the grade, which was hard work for down trains, and the tall retaining walls of the cutting between the tunnels magnified the racket produced by hard-working locomotives even into the diesel era. On the right, running along a shallow embankment, is the trackbed of the line from Church Road Junction to Birmingham Central Goods.

The Five Ways area was a direct beneficiary of the first 'Birmingham make-over' in the 1960s, which completely revitalised the area and attracted many new businesses, mainly white-collar. At that time the nearest stations were either New Street or Selly Oak, neither of which was convenient for this bustling new commercial quarter, so it was inevitable that the provision of a new station at Five Ways should be a priority in the plans for the proposed 'Cross City Line' from Redditch to Lichfield. The new station duly opened on 8 May 1978. A 10-minute-interval Cross City daytime service is now in place, fully justifying the investment in electrification and new stations. The Class 323 EMUs acquired specially for the service have now settled down and provide high availability in order to deliver the required service levels. No 323216 is seen departing for Redditch as the 1018 service from Four Oaks on 28 August 2009. Note on the right the formation of the line from Church Road Junction to Birmingham Central Goods. *Roger Shenton/JW*

CHURCH ROAD JUNCTION is of significance for two reasons, the first being that from nationalisation until 1958 it was the boundary between the newly designated Western and London Midland Regions. Second, it was the junction where the branch to Birmingham Central Goods, otherwise known as Suffolk Street Goods, diverged from the Birmingham West Suburban line. The signal box, of typical Midland Railway design, closed in September 1969. BR Standard Class 5 No 73092 is seen at the junction heading a southbound express from Birmingham New Street.

The location today is clearly identified by the distinctive brickwork on the boundary walls, although vegetation seems to be taking over the right-hand wall; this separates the railway from the Birmingham & Worcester Canal, which the railway follows as far as Lifford (see also Lifford Goods, page 65). On 5 March 2009 Class 323 No 323240 passes the site of Church Road Junction with the 0952 Lichfield Trent Valley to Longbridge service. *Peter Shoesmith/GD*

CHURCH ROAD: The railway skirts the leafy Birmingham suburb of Edgbaston and passes beneath Church Road by means of a short tunnel. The location is roughly at the summit of the climb from Birmingham New Street, which was always a challenge for trains heading south. The effort required is typified by this May 1964 view of 'Black 5' No 45263 working hard with the 5.25pm Birmingham New Street to Gloucester service.

Without the exhaust of the 'Black 5' the tunnel is visible behind Class 323 No 323217 as it emerges from the southern portal with 1118 Four Oaks to Redditch service on 5 March 2009. At this point both the railway and the adjacent Birmingham & Worcester Canal share the same cutting, with the massive brick retaining wall giving an indication of the terrain. Church Road station, which closed in 1925, was situated just beyond the northern portal at the Birmingham end of the tunnel. Note the distinctive house in the background, which over the years seems to have lost the upper part of its fire escape. *Peter Shoesmith/ GC*

SOMERSET ROAD station was to meet a similar fate to Church Road, albeit five years later in 1930, again as a result of low patronage and the need to improve pathing due to increasing congestion on the route. Ironically, the station site is right next to many of the residential blocks of Birmingham University, but when the Cross City line planners decided to opt for the site of what is now University station, about a mile to the south of this location, they no doubt also had in mind access to Queen Elizabeth Hospital. Even as early as on 30 March 1962 all trace of the station has disappeared except for what appears to be the sculptured remains of the platforms. A unidentified Class 46 rounds the curve with a southbound cross-country service for the South West.

The only tangible evidence of the existence of the station today is the different type of brickwork on the parapet of the bridge, indicating the access point to the station. The abundant woodland on the right shields the university land from the railway as Class 323 No 323218 rounds the curve with the 11.22 Lichfield Trent Valley to Longbridge service on 5 March 2009. *Peter Shoesmith/GD*

UNIVERSITY: The new station here opened on 8 May 1978 and serves both the campus of Birmingham University and the adjacent Queen Elizabeth Hospital. It affords greatly improved access to both facilities and is now one of the busiest on the Cross City line. In addition to being served by Cross City line services, some cross-country trains also call, providing better journey opportunities, particularly to the South West. The new station is under construction on 26 May 1976 as Class 45 No 45058 eases past the partly built new platforms heading the 10.40 Leeds to Plymouth service. The poplar trees form a distinctive backdrop, masking the massive Queen Elizabeth Hospital complex, whilst out of the picture on the right is the equally large campus of Birmingham University and the Birmingham & Worcester canal.

The 'present' view, taken on 11 March 2009, gives a flavour of the station today, as Cross-Country liveried Class 170 DMU No 170103 calls with the 1108 Nottingham to Cardiff Cross-Country service. *Both GD*

SELLY OAK: Following the demise of Five Ways (1944), Church Road (1925) and Somerset Road (1930), Selly Oak was for many years to be the 'fringe' station to Birmingham New Street on the Birmingham West Suburban Line. Even as late as the mid-1970s not many trains called, and the whole station was generally run down. On 28 June 1974 'Peak' No 127 heads south through Selly Oak with the 1040 Leeds to Paignton service. Note that the canopy seems to consist of the frame only, with no roof covering. Cross-platform access was by way of a subway, the entrance to which is seen just beyond the booking hall.

The launch of the Cross City line included the total rebuilding of Selly Oak, which is now a busy commuter station; the reconstruction included the provision of a footbridge to replace the dingy subway and a substantial car park befitting its commuter status. Even the background has changed beyond all recognition, as through the footbridge looms the bulk of the new Queen Elizabeth Hospital, due to open in 2010. Seen arriving on 16 February 2009 is Class 323 EMU No 323212 with the 1214 Lichfield City to Longbridge service. *Both GD*

CADBURY'S PRIVATE RAILWAY: Cadbury Brothers, whose business dates back to 1824, opened their famous factory at Bournville in 1879 on what was then a green-field site. The location had a number of attractions, one being access to clean water, and another being its situation next to both the infant Birmingham West Suburban Railway and the Birmingham & Worcester Canal. Over the years an extensive private railway network was established on Cadbury's premises, and the company was dependant on both rail and the adjacent canal for both delivery of raw materials and the distribution of its finished products. Heading along the departure road next to the main line is Cadbury No 14, a 225hp North British 0-4-0 diesel-hydraulic locomotive, which has charge of a short rake of Cadbury internal-use wagons, which, on this day in May 1976, are conveying members of the Industrial Railway Society, who are making a tour of the internal Cadbury system just prior to its closure later that month. Note one of the last surviving examples of a Midland Railway revolving signal.

The Cadbury boundary is now identified by the wire security fence, but the building just visible through the trees is the half-timbered property seen behind Cadbury No 14 in the 1976 view. On 20 February 2009 Arriva Class 220 No 220028 passes with the 0900 Bristol Temple Meads to Manchester Piccadilly service.
Peter Shoesmith/GD

CADBURY'S PRIVATE RAILWAY: The Cadbury internal system occupied both sides of the main line, which was crossed by way of an overbridge at the Birmingham end of the complex. The bridge also spanned the canal, which Cadbury used extensively until 1968. The early 1920s saw the expansion of the Waterside complex on the eastern bank of the Birmingham & Worcester Canal, which included the internal railway system. Cadbury No 1, an 0-4-0ST built by Avonside of Bristol in 1925, is seen charging along the canal wharf with a rake of main-line vans on 1 November 1962. The importance of the canal is well illustrated in this glorious view. The main line is situated behind the right-hand fence.

The scene today shows that the area is totally residential, but the location can be clearly identified by comparing the canal bank brickwork in the bottom left-hand corner, which indents at this point. Also note that the electricity pylons in the distance have not changed either. The narrow boat *Tranquillity* heads south along the Birmingham & Worcester Canal on 20 February 2009. After a period of decline, the canal system around Birmingham has been part of the city's renaissance, just as the original canal system back in the 18th century contributed to the initial prosperity and growth of Birmingham as a major industrial centre.
Peter Shoesmith/GD

BOURNVILLE: To anyone with a reasonably sweet tooth, the name of Bournville is well known throughout the world as the brand name of Cadbury's dark chocolate. The Cadbury factory is adjacent to the station, and was opened in 1879, three years after the station, which was originally known as Stirchley Street. It became Stirchley Street & Bournville in 1880, reflecting the growing importance of Cadbury's, which by this time was providing housing for its workers and the whole area was flourishing. In 1888 the names were reversed to emphasise the Bournville connection, with the final change in 1904 when Stirchley Street was dropped. The station is situated on a narrow site, hemmed in on one side by the Birmingham & Worcester Canal. The down platform is thus quite restricted, and its accommodation dates back to the early 1970s, while in this early 1960s view the up platform boasts a full canopy. Calling with a local train is Fowler Class 4 2-6-4T No 42417, probably on a service to Evesham via Redditch and Alcester. Note the Cadbury's logo placed on top of the station nameboard on the down platform.

The Cadbury connection is perhaps even stronger today, as the entire station is painted in the company's distinctive purple house colour, and Cadbury continues to be a major employer as well as providing one of the most popular tourist attractions in the area with 'Cadbury World'. The scene today is still dominated by the electricity pylon on the right, and the roof of the down platform canopy, as in the earlier view, can be seen above the roof of Class 170 No 170516, heading the 1249 Birmingham New Street to Hereford service. However, the distinctive but unattractive corrugated steel canopy, typical of the Cross City route, has replaced the traditional Midland Railway-designed waiting room and canopy on the left. *Peter Shoesmith/GD*

BOURNVILLE LOCOMOTIVE DEPOT was located to the south of the station, adjacent to the Canal Branch (see Lifford Goods, page 64), and provided much of the traction requirements for both local passenger and goods workings. Opened by the Midland Railway in 1894, initially as a sub-shed to Saltley, it gained independence in 1935, becoming '21B'. An unidentified 'Jubilee' is seen running south past the depot on an inter-regional express, and the photographer is standing within the 'four foot' of the spur from the main line providing access to the depot, the main buildings of which can be seen in the distance. The roof of Bournville signal box, located in the 'V' of the junction with the Canal Branch, is just visible above the last two coaches of the express. The lettering on the chimney stack is imploring people to 'Join the Coop'. On the far left a wagon can be seen at the summit of the inclined spur leading to the coaling stage.

The scene today could not be more different, with a recent housing development now occupying the site, which can be pinpointed by the distinctive electricity pylon that stands to the right of the house at the end of York Close. *Peter Shoesmith/GD*

43

BOURNVILLE LOCOMOTIVE DEPOT was originally equipped with a 50-foot turntable, but with the increasing length of tender locomotives a larger 57-foot version was installed in the late 1940s. Ranged around the turntable are Johnson Class 3 0-6-0 No 43523 (a class that dated back to 1885), two Ivatt Class 4 2-6-0s, Nos 43033 and 43044 (known affectionately as 'Flying Pigs', due to their reputation of being strong, fast runners but not being particularly attractive), and a Class 2P 4-4-0, No 40511 (a Fowler rebuild of an original Johnson design).

The corner of Lancaster Close and York Close is the equivalent scene today. The shed closed on 14 February 1960 and the site was originally redeveloped for industrial use. However, in more recent times, and no doubt reflecting the fortunes of the national economy, the site has seen further significant change and is now residential. *Peter Shoesmith/GD*

LIFFORD WEST JUNCTION: The Lifford Curve connects the Birmingham West Suburban line with the Camp Hill line. The latter runs from Bordesley Junction to Kings Norton, and was used as an avoiding line to keep unnecessary traffic away from Birmingham New Street station, particularly freight traffic from Lawley Street and Washwood Heath heading for Birmingham Central Goods. On 2 August 1963 Class 4 0-6-0 No 44266 on a short van train is held at the junction while Class 4 2-6-0 No 43122 heads for Birmingham New Street. Note the 60-yard Pershore Street Tunnel in the background.

The encroachment of foliage and electrification masts and wiring now dominates the scene as Class 170 No 170513 approaches with the 1239 Hereford to Birmingham New Street service on 5 March 2009. Lifford Curve survives, but does not see much traffic nowadays. Used mainly for taking empty stock workings away from New Street, it also still sees the odd passenger train looped that way for operating expediency. *Peter Shoesmith/GD*

LIFFORD WEST JUNCTION: The view north from Lifford West Junction shows its proximity to Bournville shed, which can be seen in the background, together with Bournville signal box and the 'Join the Coop' chimney (see page 42). BR Standard Class 5 No 73169 rushes south at the head of an inter-regional express on 12 December 1959, the train having the 'road' for Kings Norton, while the signals on the right-hand side of the bracket govern access to the Lifford Curve.

The key to the present scene is, again, the electricity pylon in the background. Commercial development is evident around the site of Bournville signal box, which survived until 1969. Class 323 No 323212 passes over a crossover on the approach to Lifford West Junction with the 1318 Four Oaks-Redditch service on 5 March 2009. *Peter Shoesmith/GD*

KINGS NORTON station dates back to 1849, and was situated on what was then the through route from Birmingham to Gloucester. It gained in importance with the opening of the Birmingham West Suburban Railway in 1876, which joined the Birmingham & Gloucester (by then absorbed into the Midland Railway) at the Birmingham end of the station. When opened through to New Street in 1885, the BWSR provided a quicker and more direct access to New Street, and also obviated the need for trains from the North East to the South West having to reverse. In time it became an overspill station for New Street, with its wide platforms able to accommodate crowded trains. To the south of the station there were carriage sidings on the down side together with an engineer's yard. A quite complicated track layout was required, as from Kings Norton south to Barnt Green the main line consisted of both up and down fast and slow lines. On 3 June 1963 BR Swindon Class 123 'Inter-City' four-car and three-car sets head south from Kings Norton with a Birmingham New Street to Cardiff Central service. On the left is the wooden goods shed, beyond which the fan of carriage sidings can be seen behind Kings Norton signal box, which closed in September 1969 when the route was resignalled and jurisdiction passed to Saltley Panel. Note the Midland Railway lower-quadrant stop signal on the right.

Scuttling past the scene today is Class 170 DMU No 170514 forming the 0949 Birmingham New Street to Hereford service. Although much track rationalisation has taken place, the south end of Kings Norton remains quite a complex layout and the four-track main line still extends to Barnt Green. The goods shed has long gone and the fan of carriage sidings sees little use nowadays. Before the demise of Austin Rover the sidings were utilised by car trains. *Peter Shoesmith/GD*

KINGS NORTON: On 21 July 1963 Class 9F No 92221 lumbers through the up island platform with a long train of mineral wagons, which were then so much a part of the railway scene. The train will be taking the Camp Hill line and is probably heading for Washwood Heath Yard. Note the gas lamp on the nearside platform, and that the buildings on both the island and up BWSR platforms have typical Midland Railway canopies.

Self-setting scrub is now a feature of the island platform, which has been closed to passengers for some years. It is also no longer possible to access the platforms from the footbridge, which can be seen in the distance. However, freight is still very much part of the scene at Kings Norton, although in nowhere near the volume as 40 years ago. On 7 April 2009 Advenza Class 47 No 47237 passes with empty bogie boxes from Cardiff to either Shipley or Stockton, they will return south with loaded scrap. *Peter Shoesmith/GD*

KINGS NORTON: There is much to see in this scene dating back to the late 1950s, as 'Black 5' No 44775 rumbles through Platform 1 running both light engine and tender-first, probably after depositing a rake of coaching stock in the nearby carriage siding. Meanwhile on Platform 2, which serves the down fast line, a Class 103 Park Royal two-car set has just arrived with a service from Birmingham New Street to Redditch.

The scene today shows that the platform buildings have gone, with a corrugated curved steel canopy now providing shelter on Platform 1. The scrub identifies the location of the island platform buildings, while the footbridge is now enclosed. The booking office is now at street level, to the left of the footbridge. Stopping trains still use Platform 1, although the Class 170 DMU is in fact running through with the 1040 Hereford to Birmingham New Street service on 11 March 2009. Platform 2 is not in use, and the line is used by non-stop Cross-Country services. Cross City line services now cross over at Kings Norton Junction, which can just be seen through the distant bridge, and use the platform out of view on the extreme right-hand side.
Peter Shoesmith/GD

NORTHFIELD station is situated to the south of Kings Norton on the four-track main line. The first station opened in 1870, and was replaced in 1893 with a new station consisting of an island platform serving the up and down main lines, and flanked by the up and down goods lines. A goods yard stood adjacent to the station on the up side, and the area was controlled by a signal box situated at the south end of the island platform. A local passenger train hauled by Class 4 0-6-0 No 44211 is seen easing into the up platform, while the goods yard seems to be busy judging by the number of wagons present. To the right of the loading gauge can be seen the jib of the yard's crane.

The station today has changed completely. The inception of the Cross City line in 1978 saw the island platform taken out of use, with new platforms being provided on what were the up and down goods lines. Access between the two is still by way of the subway, which used to connect to the island platform; the latter, as this scene taken on 15 April 2009 reveals, is now very derelict. The site of the goods yard is now occupied by the station car park, as Northfield is now a busy commuter station. Note also that only the outer goods lines are wired at this point. An unidentified Arriva Trains Class 220 charges north with the 14.25 Plymouth to Edinburgh service. *Peter Shoesmith/GD*

NORTHFIELD: Judging by the lack of platform activity, it suggests Hereford-based BR Standard Class 5 No 73068 is passing through Northfield at the head of a short passenger train on 8 June 1963, quite probably returning to its home base. This view shows the island platform and buildings well, with the goods yard on the left.

The nearest accessible angle today is from the new down platform, with Arriva Class 43 No 43321 at the head of the 0608 Edinburgh to Plymouth service approaching at speed and passing the remains of the island platform. Note the gables on the left, which tie in perfectly with the earlier scene. *Peter Shoesmith/GD*

NORTHFIELD: The subway that gave access to the island platform was situated at the south end, by the signal box, and its entrance can be seen in the bottom left-hand corner of this scene, which shows ex-Great Western 'Grange' 4-6-0 No 6852 Headbourne Grange on the up goods line at the head of a mixed freight on 2 May 1963.

Note the brickwork of the subway retaining wall on the extreme right-hand side of this 6 March 2009 view as Class 170 DMU No 170106 hurries the 0945 Cardiff to Nottingham Cross-Country service north through Northfield. The station is served by Cross City line services operating generally at intervals of 15 minutes. *Peter Shoesmith/GD*

HALESOWEN JUNCTION at Longbridge controlled access to both the branch to Halesowen and, more importantly, to the giant motor works established by the Austin Motor Company in 1905 which subsequently grew to be the biggest industrial complexes in the area and whose fame, or perhaps more appropriately infamy, came as much from the terrible industrial relations that beset the plant in the 1970s as from the vehicles it produced. There seems to be a bit of anticipation in Halesowen Junction signal box as an unidentified Stanier Class 8F 2-8-0 trundles past with a northbound goods on 4 December 1964. Beyond the signal box the railway enters a deep but wide cutting accommodating the four main running lines. Austin's South Works dominates the ridge of the embankment running alongside the main line. Prior to 1929 this was just a double-track railway, but the LMS decided to quadruple it as far as Barnt Green due the volume of business. As part of the widening the nearby 440-yard Cofton Tunnel was opened out, as it could not accommodate the additional lines.

The signal box closed in September 1969, but the line to Barnt Green and beyond remains busy although nowadays it is the commuter services from Redditch and Bromsgrove that dominate the traffic flows. Note the top of the water tower (top right), which survives, as does the pipework crossing the line. The absence of the now demolished South Works is hidden from view by the foliage. A strengthened 1040 Hereford to Birmingham New Street service passes on 16 February 2009 formed of Class 153 No 153363 leading an unidentified Class 170 DMU. *Peter Shoesmith/GD*

AUSTIN MOTOR COMPANY WORKS (LONGBRIDGE): This is the view looking east from the A38 road bridge into the Longbridge complex. On the left stands the North Works, which was bordered by the branch line curving around in the background to Halesowen Junction, where what looks like another of the Austin fleet of steam locomotives is shunting. To the right of the crane can be seen the roof

of the South Works, together with the roofs of houses located on the east side of the railway line. The foreground is dominated by Longbridge East signal box, while Austin No 1 is an 0-6-0ST built by Kitson in 1932; it remained in service until 1973 before passing into preservation, being now located on the Llangollen Railway. The loco is seen heading a short rake of mineral wagons on 4 April 1958.

It is a scene of dereliction today as a contractor's dumper truck passes the partly dismantled remains of Longbridge East signal box. The North Works has been demolished, as has the South Works. Note the houses on the horizon at the extreme right-hand side of the photograph, which in the earlier scene could only be identified by their roofs.

Peter Shoesmith/GD

AUSTIN MOTOR COMPANY WORKS (LONGBRIDGE): Two Austin Minis and an A40 reflect the range of what was then the British Motor Corporation (BMC) in this scene from 10 December 1962, although the presence of what looks like a Vauxhall Wyvern. On the left is the North Works while on the right the steps lead to the footbridge that ran in front of Longbridge East signal box and ultimately provided access to the station within the works, which was situated on the other side of the Bristol Road bridge. The rear of the signal box is just visible behind the footbridge steps, and the grounded goods van body behind the locomotive is that to the right of the signal box in the earlier April 1958 scene. The locomotive is Manning Wardle 0-6-0ST Abernant, built in 1921 initially for the Cardiff Bay Water Company and was purchased by the Austin Motor Company in 1927.

The demolition of the North and part of the South Works is now complete, the remains of the latter dominating the background of this March 2009 scene. Amid all the carnage note that the wall, which is not very prominent in the 1962 photograph (behind Abernant), now stands out, and even has the embedded railings still in position. The telegraph pole also has a familiar look to it! After a working life of 36 years at Longbridge, Abernant was sold for scrap, only to be rescued by Birmingham City Council for static display in a playground near Duddeston station for several years. There is a happy ending, as Abernant has been removed and is now with the Great Central Railway (North) at its Ruddington site.*Peter Shoesmith/ GD*

AUSTIN MOTOR COMPANY WORKS (LONGBRIDGE): The growth of the motor car factory and the need to get the workers to and from work prompted the Midland Railway to open a new station within the factory complex in 1915 at a point where the present A38 road crosses the line. The station was served by trains from the Halesowen branch as well as the main line. The services to the works were unadvertised, although some trains coming off the main line at Halesowen Junction were continuations of advertised services to and from Kings Norton. These trains ceased in 1960, some two years after those from Old Hill and Halesowen. On 2 May 1955 Fowler Class 4 No 42334 has charge of an evening train to Birmingham New Street. The West Works dominates the background.

The station closed with the cessation of the workmen's trains in February 1960. However, the railway remained in situ and continued to receive trains up to the closure of the works, as raw materials came in by rail as well as some finished products also leaving by rail. Clearance of the site happened as recently as 2006, and the booking hall that straddled the line remains, with both the old British Rail logo and the words 'tickets & parcels' still clearly discernable. *Peter Shoesmith/GD*

HALESOWEN: The Halesowen Railway, which opened in 1883, was in essence two separate branch lines that met in Halesowen. From Halesowen Junction on the Midland Railway the line ran through what became the Austin Motor Works, with stations at Longbridge (within the Austin Works), Rubery, Hunnington and Halesowen. The line continued west to meet the Great Western at Old Hill. Passenger services ceased in 1927, but unadvertised workmen's trains to Longbridge for the Austin factory continued until September 1958. The line was closed completely in 1964, and just prior to closure, on 2 November 1963, an SLS special traversed the line and is seen standing in Halesowen station with Ivatt Class 2 No 46522 leading.

No trace of the station remains today, as the railway formation has disappeared beneath an industrial estate. The large factory on the left-hand side on the 1963 scene remains, and is the key feature in identifying the location today. Nowadays it is hidden behind the trees that have grown up along the left-hand embankment, while the roadway now covers the trackbed. The factory has enjoyed world fame in its time, as it was where the so-called barrel of Saddam Hussein's alleged 'super gun' was cast back in 1990. *David C. Williams/JW*

RUBERY station opened in 1883 at the same time as the Halesowen branch itself, and boasted the only crossing place on the line. This is well illustrated in this view of two workers' trains on 4 April 1958, with ex-GWR 0-6-0PT No 7429 restarting a Halesowen-bound service, while classmate No 7418 heads a similar working towards the then Longbridge station, situated within the Longbridge Works complex. By this time the station had been closed for nearly 40 years, but still looks in remarkably good condition. A raft of sidings can be seen on the left-hand side, while a spur also ran to the right behind both the Midland-design signal box and station. Beyond the station at the Halesowen end, and roughly where the photographer is standing, was a gated level crossing known as Holly Hill after the minor road that crossed the railway at this point. The workers' trains through Rubery were withdrawn in September 1958.

After looking at the scene in 1958, it is difficult to believe that virtually no trace of the station and its facilities remain today. GPS coordinates (SO991/782, for anyone interested) were used to pinpoint the location, as the area has been subject to significant development and part of the site is now a nature reserve. There has been talk of heavy rail returning with a commuter service as far as Frankley, but recently this prospect seems to have dimmed. The bus stop identifies itself as the Holly Hill Shopping Centre (which is out of view behind the photographer), and the goods yard site is roughly on the left of the picture, while the location of the station is on the right, as the 1962 Ordnance Survey Map places it immediately to the north of a stream, the position of which can be identified by the crash barrier on the footpath on the far right. Note the metal post, which has stood for many years, as evidenced by its corroded base, which is almost certainly the only remaining relic of the past presence of the railway. *Peter Shoesmith/JW*

St Andrews Junction to Kings Norton

ST ANDREW'S JUNCTION: In the early days of Birmingham's railways both the Birmingham & Gloucester (B&G) and the Birmingham & Derby (B&D) ran into New Street, causing South West to North East workings to have to reverse. Until the opening of the direct route via Selly Oak, B&G trains ran via the Camp Hill line and accessed New Street via the curve between St Andrew's Junction and Grand Junction. This curve is being used in the opposite direction by Class 31 No 31286 on 29 March 1977 with a New Street to London Paddington service. Passenger trains were not a common feature at this point until the cessation of through services at Snow Hill, when London trains via Oxford and Reading were transferred to New Street. To the right is the 'Aston Curve'; opened in 1866 (around 20 years after the B&G and B&D had both reached New Street and subsequently merged to become the Midland Railway), it runs from what is now Landor Street Junction (opposite the site of Saltley shed) on an incline varying between 1 in 62 and 1 in 85 to St Andrew's Junction itself (located just behind the photographer), and at last provided a direct route that avoided reversal at New Street.

In railway terms the junction has changed little during the 30 years between these two photographs. Carrs Paints, the factory on the left, has long since been demolished and, after a period of dereliction, the land is now occupied by a smart housing development, a product no doubt of encouraging inner-city regeneration that took place around the turn of the century. The 'Aston Curve' is mainly used by freight, which in the past was usually banked as far as Bordesley Junction.. On 1 September 2001 Class 60 No 60096 Ben Macdui lifts the 1345 Saltley to Cardiff Tidal scrap train up the incline. *Both GD*

KINGS HEATH: The Camp Hill Line, as it is known nowadays, is actually the old Birmingham & Gloucester Railway through route to the South West, which became part of the Midland Railway in 1844. Until the opening of the Birmingham West Suburban Line it was the primary Midland route into Birmingham, after which it became essentially the freight bypass and secondary passenger route until 1941 when wartime operational needs prompted the withdrawal of the passenger service. Kings Heath has been a substantial suburb of Birmingham for many years, and to many people the presence of an active railway line running through the place with no passenger service is a matter of some incredulity, given the road congestion now endemic in the area. The station, which dates back to the opening of the line in 1840, was originally named after nearby Moseley, and was renamed Kings Heath when Moseley's own station opened in 1867. The goods yard survived until 1965, and on 1 September 1962 an unidentified 'Peak' heads the northbound 'Devonian' through the remains of the virtually intact station.

The obligatory retail park now occupies the location of the station and goods yard, but the Camp Hill line remains busy with both freight and cross-country passenger trains (all non-stop, of course). Proposals exist to reopen the line to local passenger trains, with the interesting plan to run a spur from the Camp Hill line to the old Great Western route in the area of Bordesley station, so that the new service would use Moor Street. That is a plan for the next decade, whereas the current order is represented by DB Schenker-liveried Class 60 No 60040 The Territorial Army Centenary, heading north past the station site with the 11.22 Westerleigh to Lindsay empty oil tanks on 9 June 2009. *Peter Shoesmith/GD*

HAZELWELL station was a relative latecomer, opening in January 1903, a feature being the platform canopies, which spanned the wide platforms. Although closed in 1941, the station remained relatively intact for some years afterwards with the canopies still in situ into the 1950s. In fact, the building on the down (southbound) platform (this is Midland Railway territory, don't forget, where up trains work towards Derby) and a good portion of the platform itself survived until quite recent times, as reflected in this 9 April 1984 scene with Class 47 No 47119 heading for the Longbridge Motor Works with a rake on empty scrap wagons.

All that remains today is a shallow embankment and a forest of trees where the station once stood. The good news is that Hazelwell, Kings Heath and Moseley are all on the list of proposed reopenings, although, perhaps of more importance, no funding has yet been allocated! On 9 June 2009 an unidentified Arriva Class 220 'Voyager' heads for New Street with the 10.00 Bristol Temple Meads to Manchester Piccadilly service. *GD/GD, courtesy of Designer Bathrooms by Michael*

LIFFORD STATION JUNCTION signal box is passed by Class 4 0-6-0 No 44160 on 2 August 1963 with a northbound freight consisting mainly of vans, probably heading for Washwood Heath Yard. In the foreground is the parapet of Lifford Lane road bridge, and the photographer is standing in the small goods yard that was located close to the site of the last of three stations, which closed in 1940, which dated back to 1885. Of the other two, one was located nearby between 1840 and 1844, while the second was located on the adjacent Lifford Goods lines (see Page 54) and existed from 1876 until 1885. On the left stands the bracket signal protecting the junction to Lifford Curve (see also Lifford West Junction, page 45).

The distinctive bridge parapet identifies the scene today, with foliage and a modern commercial premises now obscuring any view towards Lifford Station Junction. It is also interesting to note that the bridge has lost some 3 inches in the intervening years! *Peter Shoesmith/GD*

LIFFORD CANAL BRANCH was a chord from Bournville that followed the Birmingham & Worcester Canal in an arc, passing beneath the Camp Hill line before curving round to join it at a point roughly halfway between Lifford Curve East Junction and Kings Norton. With the Camp Hill line in the foreground, the interesting feature of this early 1960s scene is the background building to the left of the big tree, which is the long-abandoned second Lifford station. This was open for a relatively short period from 1876 until 1885, when it was replaced by the third station which occupied the site of Lifford's first station, on the main line just north of Lifford Curve East Junction. The Canal Branch, as its name suggests, was built as an interchange point with the Birmingham & Worcester Canal and as this scene suggests was used for a variety of goods. An unidentified diesel shunter is occupied in the yard at the head of a mixed rake of wagons.

The Camp Hill route can be seen through the now mature lineside foliage, which does leave a sufficient gap to establish that the goods yard is now occupied by industrial units. *Peter Shoesmith/GD*

LIFFORD CANAL BRANCH: Mineral wagons on the left bank of the canal pinpoint the curvature of the Canal Branch as it drops down from Lifford Goods and passes beneath the Camp Hill line. In the foreground is the Birmingham & Worcester Canal, the curvature of which the branch follows to its junction with the Birmingham West Suburban Railway at Bournville. Heading north towards Washwood Heath Yard is Stanier 'Black 5' No 44981, with steam to spare, on a goods train.

A different type of goods train is seen on 27 February 2009, as an unidentified Fastline Class 66/3 heads south with the 1052 Chaddesden (Derby) to Portbury empty merry-go-round train. It will later return north with a load of imported coal for the Midlands' power stations, which is shipped via Portbury Docks at Avonmouth. *Peter Shoesmith/GD*

LIFFORD CANAL BRANCH: The Birmingham University Railway & Inland Waterways Society special of 17 March 1962, which we have already seen on the Harborne branch, has passed through Lifford Goods and gingerly eases around the sharp curve on the Canal Branch while approaching the bridge carrying the Camp Hill line. This stark scene reflects the dereliction of the area, as by this time the canals were also in serious decline and the future for both canal and railway at this point seemed bleak. As it happens, the canal was to flourish later as a tourist amenity. The train is roughly halfway round the loop from Lifford to Bournville. In addition to the participants, who seem to be enjoying their foray onto a by then probably forgotten piece of track, photographer Peter Shoesmith was not the only one with interest in the special.

The attractive brickwork of the Camp Hill line overbridge pinpoints the scene today, together with the obligatory graffiti. The canal wharf has survived, but the trackbed is now occupied by industrial units. Close inspection of the wall, in front of which the 1962 photographers were standing, reveals that it is little altered, except for the efforts of the local vandals. *Peter Shoesmith/GD*

Proof House Junction to Birmingham International

PROOF HOUSE JUNCTION, situated to the east of Birmingham New Street, is historically important as it was created when the Grand Junction Railway from Liverpool met with the London & Birmingham Railway. It took its name from the Birmingham Gun Barrel Proof House, whose premises were, and still are, situated right next to the south side of the line on the approach to New Street; the impressive coat of arms above the entrance door makes the building unmistakable. The junction is situated just beyond the sharp gradient that lifts the line from the dip on the exit from New Street, with the lines for Aston and Wolverhampton crossing the goods lines to Curzon Street by way of a flyover, while the LNWR and Midland lines to Grand Junction stretch out ahead. On a dreary 11 May 1963 the 9.45am express from Wolverhampton High Level to London Euston gathers speed following its cautious departure from New Street with 'Duchess' No 46239 City of Chester in charge. Proof House Junction signal box is on the right.

The scene today seems to have changed considerably, although mainly due to the clutter brought about by the electrification of the route in the late 1960s. The track layout has not changed much, although it was given greater flexibility by being remodelled in 2000, as Proof House had been rightly identified as one of the biggest railway bottlenecks in the country. Today, with Curzon Street Goods closed, the 'London & Birmingham' route now sweeps beneath the flyover to Aston while trains using the flyover, which include the high-frequency Cross City North services to Sutton Coldfield and Lichfield as well as trains to Walsall and Wolverhampton, no longer face the prospect of having to cross the busy 'London lines' on the flat, which makes life a whole lot easier for the operating department. On 1 May 2009 the 13.30 New Street to London Euston service is about to pass beneath the flyover at Proof House with Driving Van Trailer No 82101 leading and Class 90 No 90019 propelling. The use of this set was due to the withdrawal of one of Virgin's Class 390 'Pendolino' trains for repair following collision damage at Willesden a few weeks earlier.
David C. Williams/JW

ADDERLEY PARK: There has been a station here since 1860, some 16 years later than neighbouring Stechford, serving the industries that progressively grew up in the surrounding area. It is also the first station on the London & Birmingham route from New Street, just 2 miles distant. This undated scene probably shows the station in the early 1960s, as there is no evidence of preparation for the forthcoming electrification of the route. The signal box at the east end of the station protected access to the goods yard, located on the city side of the Bordesley Green Road overbridge, from where this view was taken. A mixed seven-car DMU is pulling into the station with a New Street-bound service, and one passenger in particular seems to be in a hurry to get to work, judging by the open door. The cavalcade is led by a Class 103 Park Royal two-car set, with what looks like a Gloucester Railway & Carriage Class 100 two-car set sandwiched in the middle and a Class 101 three-car Metro-Cammell set bringing up the rear.

On 16 March 2009 a Class 390 'Pendolino' on a Euston to Wolverhampton service is seen passing through the station, slowing for the approach to Proof House Junction and New Street. Note that the formation of the line to the goods yard is still clearly defined. In the foreground the waiting shelter appears to have changed little; even the chip on the ridge tile (left of the chimney in the earlier view) has survived what looks like some basic roof repairs. In the background, industry seems to given way to residential development, although the large gable-ended building to the left of the background bridge survives.

Peter Shoesmith/GD

ADDERLEY PARK goods yard survived until the 1980s, in later years serving as a Permanent Way Department facility, as evidenced in the tranquil scene on 14 May 1981, as Class 25 No 25194 is seen shunting a short rake of wagons. In earlier days it would also have served the local industry, and was one of a number of local goods yards serving the districts surrounding the city centre. In the foreground is one of the ubiquitous yellow mess vans used by the PW Department, and so typical of the times.

Following closure in the late 1980s, the yard became derelict for a time before being redeveloped as an aggregate yard, as seen on 7 April 2009 as an unidentified Virgin 'Pendolino' accelerates the 1030 Birmingham New Street to London Euston service towards Adderley Park station. On the right now stands a wholesaler's single-storey unit where once stood the huge Morris Commercials motor factory, which says a lot about the current state of the so-called 'Motor City'! *Both GD*

STECHFORD is situated at the junction where the chord to Aston and the Grand Junction route north to Wolverhampton and beyond diverges from the London & Birmingham line. This line not only provides a useful means of bypassing the congested lines around New Street but also provides a useful diversionary route for West Coast services when the Trent Valley is closed. Stechford once boasted two goods yards of reasonable size, one on the up side adjacent to the station, and another on the down side to the east of the station. In this 1960s view Fowler 0-6-0 Class 4 No 44492 is easing a mixed freight out of the down-side goods yard. Note Stechford No 1 signal box in the background, which closed quite recently.

Nature and piping obscures the scene today, as an Arriva Class 158 DMU hurries by with a working from Birmingham International to Aberystwyth. The signal box has been demolished and the land behind it redeveloped for industrial use. The row of typical 1950s semi-detached houses is just discernable in the background. *Michael Mensing/GD*

STECHFORD station has changed drastically over the last 50 years. On 5 December 1959 Fowler Class 4 No 44439 draws alongside the down platform on the slow line with a mixed freight. The train will almost certainly have just left the down-side yard beyond the road bridge in the background and will probably be heading for Bescot, via the chord to Aston. At this time the station booking hall was situated on the main road bridge, just visible in the distance.

A forest of unrestricted self-setting trees now greets the traveller where the down slow lines were once situated. The retaining wall and distinctive house pinpoint the scene, but the attractive half-timbered-gabled properties, so much a feature of the 1959 scene, now struggle to make their presence felt through the abundant trees and shrubs. The station retains a good service to New Street but the junction, which once offered direct access to both the main lines as well as the station avoiding lines, is now restricted to a single-line spur that joins the main line to the east of Station Road bridge. *Michael Mensing/GD*

MARSTON GREEN is an outer suburb of the Birmingham conurbation situated next door to what was Elmdon Airport, now the greatly enlarged Birmingham International Airport. The onset of electrification is the feature of this early 1960s scene as a Class 104 DMU departs on what looks like a Birmingham New Street to Rugby stopping service. The only people to be seen are railway employees. The station has a very neat and tidy appearance, with the booking hall on the left (up) side and a similarly constructed waiting room on the down side. The footbridge does look more modern, and has possibly been altered to allow for the overhead electrification wires. The signal box also controls a level crossing, the gates being just visible at the end of the down platform.

An entirely different scene greets the visitor to Marston Green today. The station has been completely rebuilt with both the booking hall on the up side and the down-side waiting room being replaced in the style now typical of stations within the 'Centro' area. Centro, or its more modern title 'Network West Midlands', governs the integrated transport needs of the region. The level crossing has been closed together with the signal box (although the shell survived for some years after closure before demolition), and the distinctive footbridge has also been replaced by a more modern version at the Birmingham end of the station. A 'wheelchair-friendly' pedestrian footbridge now dominates the eastern end of the station. On 23 July 2009 a Class 67 is seen propelling the 1607 Shrewsbury to London Marylebone service. *Peter Shoesmith/ JW*

BIRMINGHAM INTERNATIONAL: It is quite remarkable that a pastoral scene such as this, with 'Jubilee' No 45560 Prince Edward Island heading north at the head of an unusual consist of just one 'Interfrigo' Italian refrigerated wagon and a brake-van in July 1962, could, over the next 20 years, change so dramatically. The location is the Bickenhill Lane overbridge, looking south towards Hampton in Arden. To the north is the fledgling Elmdon Airport, which is a key component in what happened next.

In the early 1970s approval was given for the construction of a new exhibition centre on the then greenfield site at Bickenhill, which was to rival the monopoly of London for major exhibitions. It was built next to the Rugby to Birmingham main line and a new station was proposed to cater for the anticipated demand for travel to the National Exhibition Centre (NEC), as it was called. The station was to provide direct access to the new exhibition centre and opened in 1976, the same year as the NEC. To provide optimum operating flexibility, in addition to the main-line platforms, up and down loops were also provided. Later, in 1984, a new terminal at the airport was opened, and a revolutionary 'Maglev' link was provided directly from the station to the renamed Birmingham International Airport; this has since been replaced by a new cable-based system. The station took the name 'Birmingham International' from the outset, and is now also an important commuter station, particularly to London Euston, with an intensive Virgin 'Pendolino' service. On 24 August Class 390 'Pendolino' No 390012 Virgin Star catches the last rays of the evening sun as it departs for New Street with the 1743 service from London Euston. *David C. Williams/JW*

Proof House Junction to Perry Barr

VAUXHALL & DUDDESTON, or just plain Duddeston as it is now known, played a significant role in the growth of Birmingham's railways – when it was opened in 1837 it was the terminus of the Grand Junction line from Liverpool. Thirty years as a goods station followed the opening of the new terminus at Curzon Street in 1839, following which the LNWR reopened the station to passengers. In time it had two island platforms, a wagon repair works on the west side and an eight-road carriage shed on the east side. Thus it remained an important station up to the 1980s, when first the carriage shed was closed, followed by the wagon repair facility. Earlier it had lost one of its platforms when the quadruple track between Proof House Junction and Aston was reduced to double track as part of economy measures instigated by British Rail in the early 1980s. This scene shows the carriage works deserted after closure.

A wider view gives a good impression of the station today, as Class 323 No 323221 departs with the 1213 Walsall to Birmingham New Street service on 1 May 2009. The station is the first out from New Street on the Lichfield and Walsall route and, like Monument Lane, was used as a 'ticketing stop' in bygone days when New Street was an open station. The booking hall, which was damaged by fire in the 1950s, remains at road level, and the overgrown state of the disused platform can be glimpsed on the extreme left. The carriage shed has been demolished and replaced by a non-railway industrial unit. The wagon repairs works have survived since closure, albeit with all access points bricked up. *Paul Dorney/JW*

ASTON is an important junction situated on the Grand Junction route from Birmingham to Wolverhampton, although nowadays it is probably better known for its proximity to Villa Park, home of Aston Villa FC. However, it remains as strategic as ever in railway terms, particularly with the line from Stechford, which connects at the eastern (Birmingham) end of the station and affords a key diversionary route for West Coast services when the Trent Valley Line is closed. Aston shed was sandwiched in the 'V' of the Stechford and Birmingham lines, while access to the short branch to Windsor Street Goods was also from the Birmingham line opposite Aston No 1 signal box, itself positioned at the entrance to the locomotive depot. At the west end is the junction to Lichfield City and Wichnor Junction, which carries the busy Cross City North trains as well as Cross-Country trains diverted from the Tamworth route due to weekend engineering work. The wooden platforms survived until the station was rebuilt as part of the Cross City electrification scheme, although the buildings had been removed much earlier and replaced with somethin of a more rudimentary construction. This early 1960s view shows a Gloucester Railway & Carriage Class 100 DMU approaching from Birmingham with a service to Walsall. The signal gantry in the background was controlled by Aston No 1 signal box; note also overhead catenery, recently erected in prparation of the lines electrification.

The position of that gantry pinpoints the scene today as the 13.07 Birmingham New Street to Hednesford service passes through the station non-stop on 27 July 2009 formed of Class 170 DMU No 170501 and an unidentified single-car Class 153 unit. Note the crossover just visible at the rear of the train, and the coach depot, which now occupies the site of Aston locomotive depot. *Peter Shoesmith/JW*

ASTON: Looking west on 28 February 1959, 'Black 5' No 45318 works through with the empty stock from a Skipton to Witton football special destined for the nearby Vauxhall carriage sidings. Burnley were the visitors at Aston Villa, and a goalless draw was the result. Aston No 2 signal box closed in July 1966 when signalling for the area was taken over by the new Birmingham New Street signal box. The junction for the Lichfield and Burton-upon-Trent line can be seen beneath the third coach.

Modernisation came to Aston with the revamp of the Cross City line, and the wooden platforms that had been a feature for so long were replaced between 1990 and 1992, together with the provision of a new booking hall and waiting room. The modern railway on 27 July 2009 is represented by the 1123 Wrexham to London Marylebone service with Driving Van Trailer No 82305 being propelled by Class 67 No 67013 Dyfrbont Pontcysyllte, provided by 'open access' train operating company Wrexham & Shropshire. *Roger Shenton/JW*

ASTON SHED was located within the junction of the line to Vauxhall & Duddeston and the Stechford Chord, and was the principal LNWR facility in the area. It mainly supplied locomotives for freight workings, although some passenger turns were also covered. The shed itself was located to the right of this scene, showing Bowen-Cooke Class 7F 0-8-0 No 49063 and an unidentified 'Black 5' standing in front of the coaling stage. The shed is bordered at the eastern end by Long Acre, on which the houses are situated. The turntable is to the left of the locomotives, situated within a fan of sidings.

The shed closed in October 1965, and the entire site has since been redeveloped as a coach and bus depot by Flights Coaches. Except for the railway, which still borders the site, all else has changed including any remnant of the locomotive depot. This 2009 view is looking eastwards from roughly the same spot as the earlier photograph, and the position of Long Acre can be pinpointed by the gable-end of the background building. *Peter Shoesmith/GD, courtesy of Flights Coaches*

WITTON station is located a mere three-quarters of a mile from Aston, and dates back to 1876. It served a number of major industrial locations in the immediate vicinity, as well as being slightly nearer to Villa Park than Aston. The importance of the surrounding industry is emphasised by this 1963 view of BR Standard Class 5 No 75054 on an up parcels train passing through the station, with the nearby head office of Imperial Metal Industries dominating the background. The industrial complex containing IMI's works was considerable, as it virtually covered a site bordering the area between Witton and Aston stations, and as far as the present M6 motorway. Witton also boasted a goods yard, which opened in 1887, and although not of any great size it survived into the 1970s.

Trees mask the demise of the IMI building, which was demolished quite recently as part of a major redevelopment of the site. The grace of the old building has been swapped for the utility of a modern flat-roofed construction, which can be seen above the Wrexham & Shropshire 1123 service from Wrexham to London Marylebone with Class 67 No 67014 pushing the three Mark 3 coaches and Driving Van Trailer No 82305. *David C. Williams/JW*

WITTON's station buildings are a bit of a curiosity, as they are of a 1950s brick and concrete design and non-standard for the area. The waiting shelter seen here, as Ivatt Class 4MT No 43022 passes with an excursion from the East Midlands to Dudley Zoo during 1963, is part of a larger block that includes the booking hall. Similar facilities exist on both platforms.

The station has changed little over the years, as this view taken on 24 August 2009 reveals. The brick and concrete station buildings remain unaltered as Class 323 No 323215 approaches with the 1447 Birmingham New Street to Walsall service. Nowadays the station is served by a 30-minute-interval service on the New Street-Walsall axis. *David C. Williams/JW*

PERRY BARR, only three-quarters of a mile north from Witton, reflects a totally different style of architecture as 'Jubilee' No 45644 Howe passes with the southbound Manchester to Bournemouth 'Pines Express' on 27 June 1956. The booking hall is situated at road level behind the photographer, but the pleasing wooden waiting rooms and facilities on the platforms add to the rural nature of the area, which, even in 1956, was a substantial suburb of Birmingham. The signal box governs the triangular Perry Barr North, South and West Junctions, so that trains can continue north to Wolverhampton on the Grand Junction, or take the left-hand fork and head for Soho and the Birmingham-Wolverhampton Stour Valley route.

Electrification and the expansion of the Birmingham road network brought about considerable changes at Perry Barr. Access to the station is still at road level, but the road itself has moved over to accommodate the needs of the automobile, and a completely new carriageway is now carried over the railway by an expanded bridge. The platforms now extend underneath the roadway at the Birmingham end, with the consequent change to the access staircases. Only basic shelters now provide accommodation on the platforms, as can be seen as Class 92 No 92009 passes with the 1555 (FO) Bescot to Wembley Yard service on 21 August 2009 with a rake of china clay slurry wagons, which complete a weekly circuit between Irvine in Scotland and France. *Michael Mensing/JW*

Cross City (North): Aston to Blake Street

GRAVELLY HILL: 'Super D' No 48930, a Bowen-Cooke-designed LNWR heavy freight locomotive, stands at the head of a Stephenson Locomotive Society special at Gravelly Hill on 2 June 1962, celebrating the centenary of the opening of the line to Sutton Coldfield. Gravelly Hill is the first station on the route from Aston and dates back to the opening of the line in 1862. Note how the authorities were much more relaxed about photography from the 'four foot' in those days.

The modern station at Gravelly Hill is a bit of the old and some of the new! The booking hall, situated behind the photographer, remains but the latticework footbridge has been replaced by an enclosed fabricated steel version to accommodate the overhead electrification. Interestingly the platform length has been cut back and inevitably the wooden platform buildings discarded. A substantial wheelchair friendly ramp now dominates the north end of the station. Heading for Four Oaks is Class 323 No 323205 forming the 1523 working from Longbridge. *Peter Shoesmith/JW*

ERDINGTON: On the eve of dieselisation, steam enjoyed a joyous swansong on the Birmingham-Sutton Coldfield route, when in 1954 push-pull working was introduced in order to speed up and add flexibility to the timetable. Increased patronage promoted pressure for more trains and push-pull was the stop-gap response until the new diesel railcars took over from March 1956. The hourly push-pull service, which ultimately extended to Four Oaks, covered that need and passenger growth on the line has continued ever since. Ivatt Class 2 No 41223 is seen pausing at Erdington on 21 May 1955 with a service to Birmingham New Street. The station had altered little since its opening in 1862.

Unfortunately, the old station buildings were swept away with modernisation and, in one instance, vandalism, when the line was electrified. Nowadays brick and tile is the order of the day, although, together with other stations modernised at the same time, the replacement buildings do have some style. Class 323 No 323216 eases into the station on 24 August 2009 forming the 1514 Lichfield City-Longbridge service. *Peter Shoesmith/JW*

WYLDE GREEN: The not-so-old order at Wylde Green in 1981 is represented by Class 45/0 No 45041 *Royal Tank Regiment* accelerating north with the 08.00 (Sundays) service from Bristol Temple Meads to Newcastle-upon-Tyne, no doubt much to the pleasure of the young lad being introduced to the fun of railway enthusiasm by a doting grandfather. The signal is Sutton Coldfield's outer home, while Chester Road, the next station south, came under the control of Erdington.

The station buildings were of a previous generation and did not survive the electrification scheme, which brought the benefits of improved passenger shelters but at the cost of the rather ghastly corrugated sheeting typical of the refurbishments on the Cross City route. Approaching the station is Class 323 No 323242 with the 1527 Redditch to Lichfield City service on 24 August 2009. *Both JW*

SUTTON COLDFIELD was the original terminus of the line from Aston, which opened in 1862, being extended to Lichfield and beyond in 1884. It was located at the end of a quite severe reverse curve, which was to have disastrous consequences in January 1955 when a diverted express derailed while passing through the station at excessive speed. This view is believed to be a few months after the accident, with the station buildings, which missed the main impact of the derailment, now restored. The booking office is situated at road level on the top storey of the building at the rear, and access to the platforms is by way of a covered walkway. The tunnel mouth is just out of sight on the right, as Ivatt Class 2 No 41223, which is working in auto-train mode, awaits departure. The station had already seen some rationalisation, as the canopy on the down side once extended the length of the platform, to match that on the up platform.

The station has not seen too much change over the years, the most significant being that the gabled building in 1955 was subsequently damaged by fire. It stood roughly where the waiting shelter is now positioned at the bottom of the walkway leading from the booking hall. The main building remains as the booking hall and principal waiting room. Note that, despite the electrification of the line, the canopy on the up platform remains fully intact. On 2 September 2009 Class 323 323243 departs with the 1133 Longbridge to Lichfield City service. *Richard Thorne collection/JW*

SUTTON COLDFIELD: The 'Car Sleeper', the forerunner of 'Motorail', was instigated in the late 1950s with services from St Austell, Newton Abbot and Sutton Coldfield to Stirling. Sutton Coldfield's service commenced on 1 June 1958 and operated through to September 1972, and was responsible for bringing some variety of motive power to a route that had been one of the first to be dieselised in 1956. The train was drawn into the platform adjacent to the goods yard, while the cars were loaded by means of a specially constructed ramp. The passenger portion of the train reversed out onto the main line, while the 'car carriers' were attached at the rear by the shunt engine. The train then headed north via Four Oaks and Lichfield to Derby, then onwards to Stirling. Standing in the car sleeper bay on 2 June 1962 is 'Super D' No 48930 with the SLS special to celebrate the centenary of the opening of the line to Sutton Coldfield.

The scene today reflects the demise of wagon-load freight, as the goods yard is now a large car park, indicating Sutton Coldfield's importance as a commuter railhead. On the left is the main station of LNWR parentage, which remain virtually unchanged, but part of the wall that separates the goods yard from the main-line platforms has been removed, together with the canopy. *David C. Williams/JW*

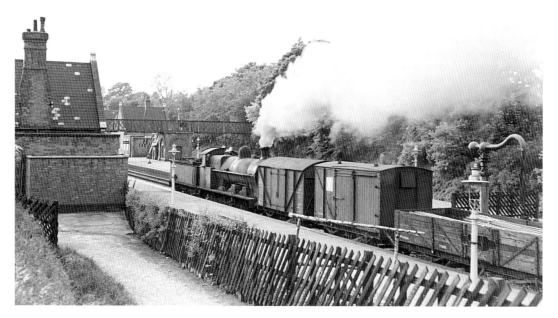

SUTTON PARK was Sutton Coldfield's second station, about 10 minutes' walk from the LNWR station and situated on the Midland line, opened in 1879, which ran, to the dismay of local residents, through the local beauty spot of Sutton Park. It was, and still is, an important route from Park Lane Junction, near Water Orton, to Ryecroft Junction on the outskirts of Walsall, which provides an effective bypass for Birmingham New Street, especially for freight. Passenger services ceased in 1965, and the line is presently used by freight and the occasional charter train. A third station existed from 1879 until 1924 at Sutton Town, but the lack of demand meant that all passenger services were concentrated at the Park station. On 30 May 1959 No 48964 is seen from the footpath access to Sutton Park station with a westbound freight.

After the cessation of passenger services the westbound station building at Sutton Park survived into the 21st century, only recently having being razed to the ground. The eastbound building fared less well, having been demolished much earlier. Local road congestion has resulted in a ground swell of opinion that the line should be reopened for passenger services, especially due to the massive expansion of housing along its entire route during the past 40 years. However, the view from the same footpath on 26 August 2009 reflects the derelict nature of the site, although the remains of the platforms can still be seen. Freight traffic continues to grow, but the return of passenger services is the news most people want to hear. *Michael Mensing/JW*

FOUR OAKS opened in 1884 when the line was extended from its former terminus at Sutton Coldfield northwards to Lichfield. In addition to an extensive goods yard, situated on the down side of the station, it also had reception sidings alongside the up bay platform, which was utilised during off-peak periods to stable DMUs awaiting the evening peak. On 17 April 1985 a Class 116 stands in Platform 2 awaiting departure with a service to Redditch, while a three-car Class 116 occupies Platform 3 and two six-car Class 116 sets are positioned in the two carriage sidings. The semaphore signals had been replaced by colour lights a few years earlier and the old latticework footbridge has by now been replaced by a utilitarian metal bridge, which was the first indication that electrification was on its way. Of note here is the classic LNWR booking hall and waiting room, which retained the distinctive flat canopy that has survived into the electrification era.

Twenty years on the basic scene has changed little. The clutter of electrification intrudes, but the station buildings remain intact and, more importantly, cared for. The carriage reception sidings have been torn up, but bay Platform 3 remains and is used for two trains each hour that turn round at Four Oaks. The signal box closed with electrification, when the entire line came under the control of Aston signalling centre, located at Duddeston. An extensive car park now occupies the site of the goods yard on the down side. The position of the colour light in the earlier scene, together with the semaphore that it replaced, can be identified by the respective concrete blocks into which the posts were secured. On 23 May 2009 Class 323 No 323213 has just arrived with the 1533 service from Longbridge to Lichfield City, while in the bay No 323222 is ready to depart with the 1618 to Redditch. *Both JW*

BUTLERS LANE is a recent addition to the Cross City line, if you regard 1957 as being recent – some 70 years later than its immediate neighbours of Four Oaks and Blake Street. The line had been 'dieselised' the previous year and the new station catered for the increased demands of commuters for access to central Birmingham following the rapid expansion of housing north of Sutton Coldfield during the 1950s and beyond. Growth has been a constant theme: starting as an unstaffed halt, the station soon became a staffed halt, the original facility being constructed entirely of wood. A complete rebuild was undertaken in 1992 at the time of electrification. The basic nature of the station is well illustrated in this 17 April 1985 view, as prototype Metro-Cammell Class 151 DMU No 151001 calls while under evaluation. Note the wooden platforms and the basic waiting shelter.

In 1992 the old station was completely swept away, forcing its temporary closure for several weeks, and the modern replacement now boasts a purpose-built booking hall and waiting room, all of brick construction, while both platforms have been totally reconstructed in concrete. Class 323 EMU No 323243 is seen with a 1544 Lichfield City to Longbridge service on 23 May 2009. *Both JW*

BLAKE STREET is the most northerly station within the present West Midlands county, and dates back to 1884. For most of its existence it was in a rural landscape; the encroachment of new housing north of Sutton Coldfield that commenced in the 1950s was not finally to envelop the Blake Street area until the late 1970s. This relaxed scene looking north towards the station on 3 March 1962 shows the railway as it once was, with each station having its own goods yard. The signal box, which closed the following day, faces the goods shed with wagons awaiting collection by the daily pick-up freight. Note the expanse of the goods yard, with what looks like an old suburban coach hard against the buffers on the left. The station, in the background, sports typical LNWR canopies on each platform. However, the total absence of any sort of major development is the most striking feature of this view, because it was all to change – and how!

If it were not for the dreaded leylandii trees, the scene today would be revealed as being fully built up, with major housing developments surrounding the station. Indeed, the view from the Hill Hook road bridge has little resemblance to that sylvan 1962 vista, as Class 323 No 323241 departs with the 15.22 Lichfield Trent Valley to Longbridge service on 23 May 2009.
Roger Shenton/JW

Grand Junction to Whitacre Junction

SALTLEY MOTIVE POWER DEPOT: A motive power depot has existed on the Saltley site, next to the down line, since 1868, in addition to the already established shed on the opposite side of the line, itself now closed, on the site of what was to become Lawley Street Goods Station. The Saltley site was progressively expanded so that by 1900 there were three roundhouses on the site, at which date Lawley Street shed closed. It was the major Midland Railway depot in Birmingham, and second only to Derby. It survived until the end of steam in Birmingham, then became a traction maintenance depot covering the diesel traction requirements of the area. It is in this guise that we see Saltley on 9 December 1986, showing the variety of traction then available. Class 50 Nos 50041 Bulwark and 50019 Ramilles together with an unidentified 'Peak' Class 45 await their next passenger turn, while the freight sector is represented by a quartet of Class 58s, headed by No 58045. Representatives of Classes 47 and 56 can be seen on the extreme left.

The reduced demand for locomotive haulage since the turn of the century signalled the decline of Saltley, and inevitably the end came in 2006 when the maintenance facility closed. The buildings, which were a product of a mid-1960s modernisation of the depot, remain, but the yard is becoming progressively overgrown. The vantage point for these photographs is an industrial estate alongside the depot, which was once part of the greater steam depot. The Lickey Incline Class 66 banking locomotive is still reported to be stabled here. Upon closure of the depot the fuelling point was transferred to the nearby Washwood Heath Yard. *Both GD*

SALTLEY station consisted of an island platform situated between the up and down running lines immediately to the north of Saltley Viaduct, so called as it carries a major road over the expanse of railway at this point. On a cold day BR Standard Class 5 No 73155 struggles with what looks like a heavy train of concrete sleepers, most probably just out of the nearby Washwood Heath Yard. Although sunny, it looks likely that the picture was taken quite early, as the gloom of the background has not yet dissipated. Lurking in that gloom can be seen Saltley Sidings signal box.

The location today can be identified by the distinctive retaining wall, although part has now been replaced by metal railings that now border so much of our railway system. Saltley station closed in 1968, so nowadays Water Orton is the first station out of Birmingham on the old Midland route. Nonetheless this continues to be a busy section of line for both passenger and freight, as this scene suggests. An Arriva Cross-Country working speeds north consisting of a Class 220/221 'Voyager' set while DB Schenker (previously EWS) Class 66 No 66030 approaches with the 1010 Corby to Margam steel train. The set of wagons on the right is the stone empties for Peak Forest. *Peter Shoesmith/GD*

SALTLEY: On a clearer day a couple of Ivatt Class 2 2-6-0s provide the interest from the north end of Saltley station on 25 July 1964. No 46448 is likely to be reversing from Saltley shed to Washwood Heath Yard for a freight turn. In the background are the cooling towers of Nechells Power Station and the gasometers from which Birmingham at this time derived most of its power. Standing proud in front of the cooling towers is Saltley Sidings signal box, which closed in 1969 when control of the route was transferred to the new Saltley Power Box.

Access to the station site is no longer possible, but this photograph is taken from Saltley Viaduct roughly at the point of the entrance to the station. Nechells Power Station has long since closed and the site is now occupied by part of the M6 motorway and Star City, an entertainment complex. The gasometers survive, as after the massive Saltley Gas Works closed they were retained to store the natural gas from beneath the North Sea, which replaced town gas. Approaching the site of the station is Arriva Class 170 No 170113 working the 1216 Leicester to Birmingham New Street service on 16 March 2009. *Peter Shoesmith/GD*

NECHELLS POWER STATION: The Central Electricity Generating Board's Robert Stephenson & Hawthorn 0-6-0T No 3 (Works No 7537 of 1949) hauls a rake of mineral wagons within the Nechells Power Station complex. The wording on the locomotive's water tank says 'Central Electricity Authority, Midlands Division'. This was one of four locomotives the CEGB maintained at Nechells, and following the closure of the power station this locomotive, and a sister engine, were preserved on the 'Battlefield Line' heritage railway based at Shackerstone in Leicestershire.

The brickwork forming the retaining walls of the Birmingham & Warwick Junction Canal pinpoint the scene today, together with the distinctive abutment of the bridge carrying the pipe over the canal. Note, too, the wrought iron gate and fencing on the extreme left-hand side, which has survived all the changes that have taken place at this location. *Peter Shoesmith/GD*

BROMFORD BRIDGE: This is the scene looking from Bromford Lane bridge in 1963, while steam still dominated the works and the M6 was just a twinkle in the planner's eye! What is believed to be Hawthorn Leslie 0-4-0ST Wellingborough No 3 (Works No 3813 of 1935) scuttles along with a single mineral wagon. Stocks of steel tube lie awaiting collection, some of which look suspiciously like lamp posts. In the background is Bromford Bridge Oil Depot, which exists through to the present day.

The M6 now dominates the location today, together with the new bridge carrying the Birmingham Inner Ring Road, which forms part of a traffic island that includes the old Bromford Bridge. The site of the steel works is now part of an industrial estate, and the sidings area is now storage space. *Both GD*

WASHWOOD HEATH YARD: Freight sidings were first established at Washwood Heath, on the down side of the main line, in 1877. Further expansion took place before the turn of the century, but a presence on the up side did not happen until 1918. The growth of industry in the area required further expansion to take place on the up side in the 1930s. The yard's growth and importance was due to its location, being both close to the centre of Birmingham and also astride the main line, and continued into the 1970s until the decline in wagon-load traffic signalled the start of its decline. This photograph, dating back to the mid-1960s, is important as it shows the full extent of the up yard before the advent of the M6 motorway, which now runs parallel to the railway at this point. A pair of Southern Region-based Class 33s are seen passing on the main line with a train of four-wheel oil tanks from Fawley refinery near Southampton to the nearby Bromford Bridge Depot. Looming out of the misty background is Nechells Power Station and the gasometers of the local Saltley Gas Works.

The yard has been progressively downgraded over recent years, and has ended up being a convenient place to stage block workings, such as cars for import and export, intermodal traffic and merry-go-round coal trains. This view from Bromford Lane overbridge changed substantially some years back with the opening of the Birmingham Spine Road, part of the city's inner ring road, which spanned the yard at this point. For a short time it also became a fuelling point for EWS locomotives following the closure of nearby Saltley. Now, though, all this is gone and the yard closed in 2009. The proximity of both the M6 and the Spine Road are clearly evident as Class 170 No 170639 speeds past with the 1639 Birmingham New Street to Nottingham service on 12 May 2009. *Peter Shoesmith/GD*

CASTLE BROMWICH is in the heart of the major industrial area east of Birmingham, which has for many years been associated with two icons of British design and engineering: Jaguar Cars, whose works are situated close to the Midland main line between Bromford Bridge and Castle Bromwich, and the Spitfire aircraft, many of which were built and tested on the nearby airfield, which also abutted the railway. Indeed, the Castle Bromwich plant manufactured more than half the Spitfires constructed during 1939-45, as well as a significant proportion of Lancaster bombers. In its time the airfield was used extensively for both commercial and military purposes and survived until 1958. Also within its boundary was the British Industries Fair, an annual exhibition in the 1950s and a forerunner of the National Exhibition Centre. Just down the road from the site of the station is a major steel sculpture entitled 'The Sentinel' by Tim Tolkien, which celebrates the local connection with the Spitfire. The aerodrome was sold for housing and is now occupied by one of Birmingham's largest estates, known as Castle Vale. Suffice to say, the area remains vibrant today with a mixture of industry, retail parks and housing, so it is perhaps a little surprising that the railway station closed in 1968 after some 126 years of service. The wide platforms are well in evidence as 'Patriot' No 45519 Lady Godiva passes with the northbound 'Devonian' on 5 September 1959.

While not a current scene, this 1984 view remains representative of the scene today, except for the addition of an extra carriageway to the Tyburn Road overbridge. All trace of the station has been swept away except for the far up slow line platform, whose brick fascia remains. Class 45 No 45126 heads east at the head of a rake of Mark 1 coaches forming a Birmingham to Leicester football special for Aston Villa supporters on 27 October 1984. They would return unhappy following a 5-0 defeat! *Michael Mensing/JW*

WATER ORTON is now the first station out of Birmingham New Street on the ex-Midland Derby and Nuneaton route, and is the point where the two lines diverge. The East Junction signal box controlled the movements over this important junction, which was a lot more complex than today as this mid-1960s view shows. The 'old' route via Whitacre bears off to the right, while the 'new' fast route, a cut-off via Lea Marston to a new junction near Kingsbury, opened in 1909. This also resulted in a new station being built, replacing the original split-platform structure that dated back to 1842. Of further interest is the massive Hams Hall Power Stations complex on the horizon. In all, three separate power stations occupied the site, the first dating back to 1905. Hams Hall 'A' was the first to close in 1975 and its cooling towers were demolished in 1978. The 'B' station, opened in 1942, survived until 1981, and the 'C' station ran from 1958 until 1992. This scene pre-dates the demolition of the 'A' station towers and shows an unidentified Sulzer Type 2 (later Class 25) taking the direct route to Tamworth with a van train.

Water Orton is as busy as ever today with a regular flow of both passenger and freight traffic, the latter having particularly increased following the development of a huge railfreight terminal on the site of Hams Hall Power Stations together with the growing importance of the nearby Birch Coppice terminal on the site of the old colliery of the same name. With the closure of East Junction signal box in the late 1970s, the layout was rationalised so that Nuneaton-bound traffic now runs 'wrong line' on the bi-directional down main line through the station to the junction. On 25 August 2009 Class 170 No 170637, forming a Cross-Country service from the East Midlands, has just crossed the junction onto what is the bi-directional track on the approach to Water Orton. The footbridge, which has quite a lengthy span, was removed and refurbished a few years ago. Unfortunately, the same cannot be said of the station, situated behind the photographer, as although the shell of the booking hall remains it is now in a sorry state of repair. *Peter Shoesmith/JW*

COLESHILL: What is now Coleshill Parkway, situated between Whitacre Junction and Water Orton, began life in 1842 as Forge Mills for Coleshill, shortened to just Forge Mills in 1904, most likely in recognition that the town of Coleshill was some distance away. Some time later life became a little complicated, as a Coleshill station already existed on the line from Whitacre Junction to Hampton in Arden, which had closed to passengers in 1917 and eventually to freight in 1939. In 1923 that station had been renamed Maxstoke, and remained open for goods traffic, while Forge Mills became Coleshill, the name it retained until closure in 1965. The substantial station building looks reasonably well maintained in this early 1960s view, which shows a three-car Class 104 DMU heading for Birmingham.

In the intervening years a number of key developments have taken place that have had a significant impact on Coleshill, and ultimately led to the reopening of the station. The 'Parkway' name is significant, and recognises the importance of the nearby M42 motorway, which has key links to the national motorway network, and the combined impact of the National Exhibition Centre and adjacent Birmingham International Airport. All these influences have bought business to the area, and the station also provides an ideal gateway for passengers travelling on the cross-country route from Birmingham to East Anglia. The modern station incorporates a bus interchange with direct routes to the NEC and the airport as well as a good-sized car park, which has not escaped the vision of rail charter operators who now frequently use the new station as a pick-up/set-down point for their tours. On 25 August 2009 Class 170 No 170114 is seen departing with the 1116 Leicester-Birmingham New Street service. *Peter Shoesmith/JW*

WHITACRE JUNCTION station was a substantial affair considering its rural location, as illustrated in this view as the 9.35am Leicester London Road to Birmingham New Street service, formed of a Gloucester Railway Carriage & Wagon Class 104 and Metropolitan-Cammell Class 101 combination, winds around the reverse curve on 5 May 1963. On the extreme right is the original Birmingham & Derby line, which, when opened in 1839, continued to Hampton in Arden on the London & Birmingham Railway. A more direct line to Lawley Street opened in 1842 and with it the first Whitacre station at a point roughly three-quarters of a mile from the its successor. The latter opened in 1864 together with the line to Nuneaton, which can be seen curving away to the right beyond the station. The branch to Hampton in Arden lost its passenger service in 1917 and closed for freight in 1935, although it was used for the storage of wagons until the 1950s. Note the raft of sidings to the right of the station building, following the curve of the Nuneaton line.

The layout at Whitacre has changed little over the years, and the station site can be clearly identified from the void between the main and former station loop line. The latter was until recently used as a run-round facility, hence the provision of lighting, but the location of a public right-of-way foot crossing beyond the curve on the Nuneaton line has curtailed this activity. The old main line is now used as a secondary route to keep freight clear of the busy Birmingham to Derby main line, which now runs directly from Water Orton to Kingsbury Junction. The line is now busier than ever with freight traffic due to the opening of two major freight-handling facilities at Hams Hall and Birch Coppice. On 24 August Class 56 No 56312 slows in readiness for the crossover from the main line into Hams Hall with the 1200 Intermodal service from Dollands Moor. *Michael Mensing/JW*

Birmingham Snow Hill

BIRMINGHAM SNOW HILL station opened in 1852 when the Great Western's broad-gauge line was extended from Oxford to Birmingham. Originally known alternatively as 'Livery Street' or 'Great Charles Street', it officially became 'Snow Hill' in 1858. The initial basic station was rebuilt in 1871 to reflect the growing importance of Birmingham as both a commercial and industrial centre. This new station consisted of two elliptical overall-roofed train sheds at the rear of the majestic Great Western Hotel, reported at the time to be one of the finest in the land. Traffic using the station continued to grow and in 1906 this was recognised with a scheme to rebuild the station to meet future projections. The rebuilding process took two years without disruption to traffic and the result was arguably one of the finest stations ever built. This view dates from the rebuilding period of 1910-12 and shows a 'Badminton' Class 4-4-0 amidst the iron and steel framework of the new stations. Note the girders of Great Charles Street bridge on the right-hand side, an enduring feature of the location to the present day.

A Chiltern Railways Class 168 'Clubman', No 168004, stands in Snow Hill awaiting departure with the 1212 service to London Marylebone on 12 June 2009. It is standing just ahead of the Great Charles Street bridge girders, which have been modified through the years. The northern portal of the new station intrudes, while in the distance is the construction site for the station's new northern entrance. *GD collection/GD*

BIRMINGHAM SNOW HILL: At the south end of Platform 7 around 1964, the most telling feature is the presence of a 'Western' diesel-hydraulic locomotive, No D1008 Western Harrier, on a Paddington express, as the 'Kings' had been withdrawn in 1962. Central to the scene are the two schoolboys, who are no doubt discussing the various merits of diesel and steam traction, while others seem to be deep in thought or anticipation. Snow Hill Tunnel looms ahead; although presenting no issues for up trains, down trains, especially heavy freight workings, had to contend with a 1 in 45 gradient. In chambers connected to the tunnel were stables for the horses that shunted wagons around the station's fish platforms (Birmingham boasts one of the country's best fish markets to this day), the pantry for provisions for the restaurant cars, and a direct connection to the nearby Bank of England, which was served by bullion trains.

Platform 3 in the new station, extends over the track where D1008 stood on the old station. The new station is totally utilitarian and, although open to the elements on each side, the interior is still dark and not particularly welcoming. Although when reopened it had four platform faces, the lines to the left are now occupied by the Midland Metro services, which terminate at Snow Hill. However, a plan to extend the Metro lines into the city centre may once again open up this platform for heavy rail use, and provide Snow Hill with much-needed additional capacity. In the background a Class 150 DMU emerges from Snow Hill Tunnel with the 1442 Shirley to Kidderminster service on 2 June 2009. *Peter Shoesmith/GD*

BIRMINGHAM SNOW HILL: The mighty girders supporting the roof of the old station are well illustrated in this scene featuring Old Oak Common's 'Castle' No 5090 Neath Abbey on an up breakdown train on 16 March 1962. The train is standing on the up through road awaiting a path. One of the characteristics of Snow Hill was the excellence of the buildings, which were constructed of salt-glazed wall bricks, blue-pressed Staffordshire bricks and buff terracotta cornices. Each of the main platforms were topped off with huge clocks, which were visible throughout the station, as evidenced in this scene confirming the time as 1.05pm.

It is not quite the bright inviting scene at the same location today, as the gloom of the interior of the new Snow Hill is clearly evident, even though it is only 11.05 in the morning. Class 150 No 150014 will shortly proceed south forming the 10.26 Kidderminster to Shirley service, while on the left is a glimpse of a Class 165 DMU on the 1112 Chiltern service to London Marylebone. *Peter Shoesmith/GD*

BIRMINGHAM SNOW HILL: Was it a cop, or wasn't it? The young trainspotter's face gives little clue as he walks away from a scene of activity on Platform 6 following the arrival of Oxford-based 'Castle' No 5025 Chirk Castle with a down express on 12 April 1962. Parcels have already been unloaded from the guard's compartment, and note also the trolleys stacked with boxes on the extreme right, reflecting a scene once very common at railway stations. This scene also gives a good impression of the scale of the ironwork used when the station was reconstructed between 1910 and 1912.

The girders of Great Charles Street bridge present the only clue to the location today, as Chiltern Railways Class 168 'Clubman' DMU No 168003 emerges from the gloom of the new Snow Hill with the 1320 service from London Marylebone on 23 June 2009. Where there were once four tracks running through the centre of the station, there are now but two, with the platforms being extended over what were once the up and down platform roads. The DMU is standing on the equivalent of the down centre road of the old station. Also, in place of the lofty roof, which let in plenty of light, there is now a car park. *Peter Shoesmith/GD*

BIRMINGHAM SNOW HILL: Unlike its neighbour New Street, Snow Hill saw also a considerable amount of freight traffic. On 30 April 1957 Chester-based 'Grange' No 6806 Blackwell Grange awaits the road at the extreme north end of Platform 6 with a down freight consisting mainly of box vans. Although an 'airy' station, Snow Hill was built within a confined location, which resulted in the two main island platforms extending to just over 1,200 feet. By means of scissors crossovers midway along each platform, each could accommodate two trains, and the rear one was able to leave ahead of the one in front if necessary. Note also the distinctive front end of an AEC railcar glimpsed on the extreme right, probably on a Dudley service. These were introduced by the Great Western for low-volume suburban and rural services from 1934 onwards.

The ever-expanding Birmingham city centre skyline dominates the scene from what would have been the end of the old Platform 6, in effect dwarfing the station. Note, too, the development of a new northern entrance to the station (from Great Charles Street), which is intended to improve access for passengers using the station from the flourishing Jewellery Quarter side of the city. The one item that spans the 52 years between these two scenes is the spire on the left, clearly outlined in 1957 but showing just the tip on the far left hand side. The 1427 Stratford-upon-Avon to Stourbridge Junction service formed of Class 150 No 150016 threads its way north amidst the architectural variety of Birmingham in June 2009. *Michael Mensing/GD*

BIRMINGHAM SNOW HILL: A classic scene looking north towards the station throat as Old Oak Common's No 6018 King Henry VI arrives with the 2.40pm Birkenhead to London Paddington express on 9 May 1958. By this date the coaching stock reflects the change of livery that was in progress, presenting both the new maroon livery and the older, and individual Western Region livery, of chocolate and cream. The confines of the location are well illustrated, even down to the economical use of space by balancing the distinctive Snow Hill North signal box on a narrow base. Note the intricate layout, a feature of the times but very rare nowadays. The canopy is that at the end of Platform 6, and the train is easing up the 1 in 47 gradient having just passed beneath the north end of Livery Street and the Hockley Tunnels.

The modern railway intrudes at this location today, as a forest of junction boxes and a speed restriction sign dominate the scene looking north from the end of what is now Platform 2. However, study the buildings and a couple of familiar shapes are still present, like the gabled factory roof above the second coach of No 150001, which is easing into Snow Hill with the 1047 Worcester Foregate Street to Shirley service, and the distinctive building with three chimneys and a spired tower that stands behind what is St Paul's Metro stop. *Peter Shoesmith/GD*

BIRMINGHAM SNOW HILL: This unusual early-1960s view of the northern throat of Snow Hill was taken from the suburban platform on the eastern (up) side of the station. The lines to the left ran into the bay Platforms 9 and 10, while that running to the right was a loop that ran through Platforms 11 and 12 and rejoined the main lines just inside Snow Hill Tunnel. A similar arrangement existed on the down side. A Class 116 DMU approaches from the north on a suburban service while 'Hall' No 7918 Rhose Wood Hall is on pilot duties, which it will be sharing with a pannier tank, the latter being utilised for trip workings around the station, as there were extensive goods facilities located within it.

The scene today is viewed from the construction site next to the new station, which is considerably redeveloping the area and will no doubt increase the patronage of the station. Saplings have taken over the goods yard where the 'Hall' was positioned, and to the left is the Metro line into the station. If proposals for diverting the Metro into the city centre come to fruition, the diversion will be in this area, with a route via Colmore Row via Corporation Street and into New Street for a terminus at Victoria Square. *Peter Shoesmith/GD, courtesy Harrington Construction*

BIRMINGHAM SNOW HILL was a casualty of the London Midland West Coast electrification scheme, which concentrated services on the New Street to Euston route and came on stream on 6 March 1967, coinciding with the withdrawal of main-line services from Snow Hill. A year later the tunnel between Snow Hill and Moor Street closed, leaving only the services to Wolverhampton Low Level and the Black Country to stagger on until the axe finally fell and the last train ran on 6 March 1972. The Great Western Hotel had been demolished in 1969, and after closure the station remained intact for some while being utilised as a car park. However, years of neglect finally took their toll, and a survey revealed many areas of the station to be in a dangerous condition; demolition commenced in 1976. The end is nigh as a Class 121 'bubble car' stands in Platform 4 in early March 1972. The through lines, domain of the 'Kings' and 'Castles', have been lifted, while in the foreground are the girders of the Great Charles Street bridge.

The local transport authority had plans to open an east-west cross-city line following the success of the original Lichfield-Redditch Cross City line, and trains returned to a rebuilt Snow Hill through a re-opened tunnel in September 1987; a through connection to the Stourbridge line at Galton Junction was re-established in 1995 and the Metro tram system between Snow Hill and Wolverhampton St George's opened in 1999. The Snow Hill of today consists of three platforms (the fourth is used for Metro services), which are fully occupied on 23 June 2009 as, on the right, Class 150 No 150009, forming the 1522 Shirley to Worcester Foregate Street service, awaits departure. The car park that sits on top of the station, while functional, does the city no favours due to its lack of any architectural merit. *Both GD*

BIRMINGHAM SNOW HILL: It is only when Snow Hill is viewed from afar that the true scale of the place is revealed. Although hemmed in on both sides, this distant view from the north end of Livery Street in April 1968 gives a graphic indication of its sheer size, and the complexity of the track layout. The parapet of the overbridge on Livery Street is in the right foreground and the main lines can be seen descending beneath the bridge. To the left is a raft of sidings, while in the background the platform capacity is evident, although it must be remembered that the platforms actually extended for equally as far beneath the overall roof. A lone 'Toad' brake-van stands forgotten amidst the desolation, while the 'new' Birmingham, in the shape of the Rackhams building on the right and West Midlands Police Headquarters on the left, is a foretaste of the future.

The scene today shows that all was not lost. When the route to Wolverhampton closed, it was a condition that the trackbed was left intact, thus opening up the opportunity years later for the Midland Metro and the Jewellery Line. Snow Hill itself is getting busier, and the reopening of the terminal platforms at Moor Street will go some way to easing current congestion. The striking feature of the scene today is the sheer scale of the redevelopment, mainly commercial, within the vicinity of the station, which means that future growth and prosperity is assured. On 17 December 2008 DMU No 150104 climbs the steep gradient from the Hockley Tunnels into Snow Hill with the 0926 Kidderminster to Dorridge service. The Metro tracks are on the left, while away on the right is the stabling point for DMUs between turns, which today is essential so as not to take up platform space unnecessarily. *Both GD*

109

Snow Hill to Galton Bridge

HOCKLEY/JEWELLERY QUARTER: Hockley station is in the middle distance of this wonderful panoramic scene on 5 May 1964 from Vyse Street as 'Manor' No 7821 Ditcheat Manor (now preserved and based at Oswestry) drifts towards Birmingham Snow Hill light engine. The scale of the goods yard and facilities is quite breathtaking, and of importance due to its proximity to the significant local industry, which includes Birmingham's famous Jewellery Quarter. The ever-growing dominance of road freight and the greatly improved national road links focused on Birmingham, together with the downgrading of the Great Western main line through the city, all contributed to the demise of Hockley, with the yard closing in 1967, followed by the station in 1972. Note the city's Key Hill Cemetery on the right, which is the last resting place for many well-known local dignitaries including members of probably Birmingham's 'first family', the Chamberlains. Unfortunately, the Doric-style temple was deemed unsafe and demolished two years after this picture was taken.

The view from Vyse Street on 15 April 2009 today is dominated by the new Jewellery Quarter station, which reflects the changing influences within the area and has been sited centrally to the vibrant Jewellery Quarter of the city. The left-hand tracks are Network Rail's Jewellery Line from Snow Hill, and the roof of a Class 150 DMU can be seen as it heads towards the tunnels that lead through to Snow Hill. On the right are the Metro tracks, with Tram 02 standing at the Metro station. *Peter Shoesmith/GD*

SOHO & WINSON GREEN: A '5100' Class 2-6-2T 'Prairie' tank heads away from Soho & Winson Green station on 13 April 1962, and is about to pass beneath the ex-LMS line that forms a loop to the north-west of Birmingham, running between the triangular junctions at Perry Barr and Soho; two stations were situated on this line, at Soho Road and Handsworth Wood, both of which closed in 1941. The sidings in the foreground form part of Winson Green Goods Depot, which was one of the major goods facilities in the area.

In the intervening years between these two photographs the formation of the old Great Western route lay derelict, but now a four-track formation is again in situ. The two far tracks are used exclusively by the Midland Metro trams, and No 12 is seen approaching Soho Benson Road (Foster Gardens) tram stop with a working from Wolverhampton St George's to Birmingham Snow Hill on 6 March 2009. The ex-LMS route can be seen in the background, now electrified. *Peter Shoesmith/GD*

Opposite left: **Looking through the glass window of Jewellery Quarter station's footbridge shows how the area surrounding what was Hockley station and goods yard has changed. A new factory now occupies a large proportion of the southern end of the yard, while the area to the extreme left (out of view) is now an industrial estate; all that remains of the railway is the high brick retaining wall next to Pitsford Street. Of the multiple tracks, just the four running lines used by the Jewellery Line and Midland Metro remain. Class 150 No 150106 forms the 1529 Great Malvern to Shirley service on 15 April 2009, while a Metro Tram approaches from Wolverhampton.** *GD*

HANDSWORTH & SMETHWICK: A pair of English Electric Type 4s (later Class 40s) are not quite what you would expect to see on the Great Western main line near Handsworth & Smethwick station in 1965. The year is the key, however, as Euston, Birmingham New Street and Wolverhampton High Level services were being diverted due to the electrification work taking place on the Stour Valley route. This bought a short-term gain to the ex-GW route, although ultimately its demise, when the commencement of electric services the following year resulted in the former losing its through express services

to London and the south. No D236 leads a relatively light load for the double-header along what is now the tram tracks for the Midland Metro. The station can be seen in the background, with its footbridge spanning all four running lines. On the right is the goods yard that serves both the local industry and, no doubt, the demands for domestic coal by the local population.

The station closed in 1972, together with the remnants of the main line between Wolverhampton Low Level and Birmingham Snow Hill, but a stub remained open from Galton Junction as far as Handsworth for the cement terminal and scrapyard, the latter occupying the site of the old goods yard. The remaining line followed the course of the old down road to Stourbridge as Class 37 No 37198 heads back to Bescot, via a reversal at Langley Green Yard, with a consist of scrap from Coopers scrap merchants and cement from the Blue Circle terminal on 6 August 1990. The remains of the station's down platform can be seen in the background, and the gable-ended factory and large factory building, which can be seen on the left of the 1965 scene, also survives. *Michael Mensing/JW*

By 1996, the date of the third view, the Jewellery Line had been reinstated and except for extra security fencing at Coopers scrap yard the only major, and significant, change is the preparation of the trackbed for the Midland Metro. The station site has been cleared, beyond which can be seen the spur running into the scrapyard, which still despatches scrap trains to this day. Note the curve of the main line and the expanse of the cleared site, as the Metro will cross the Jewellery Line on a flyover at this point. Making a change from the normal Class 150s are Class 37 No 37207 leading Class 31 No 31439 on 'The Jewel in the Crown' railtour en route from Stratford-upon-Avon to Worcester on 24 February 1996.

The scene today reflects the busy commuter route that both the Jewellery Line and the Metro have become, the former having a roughly 15-minute-interval service from Snow Hill to Stourbridge Junction, while the latter runs at intervals of between 8 and 10 minutes. The Metro stop is named 'Handsworth Booth Street' and is situated at the base of the flyover that carries the Metro over the Jewellery Line. Heading for Kidderminster on 5 August 2009 is the 1442 service from Shirley formed of two Class 150 DMUs, with 'Network West Midlands'-liveried No 150126 leading. *Both JW*

THE HAWTHORNS, or Hawthorns Halt as it was otherwise known, took its name from the nearby West Bromwich Albion football ground, which the station served from Christmas Day 1930 until closure on 29 March 1968. Situated at Handsworth Junction, it opened on match days only. The station was of a very rudimentary nature as the Great Western had resisted overtures from 'The Albion' for a more convenient station for some time. However, in its time it was heavily used on match days, catering for excursion traffic as well as local workings that called additionally here on such days. On 25 March 1961 scruffy 'Black 5' No 44907 heads towards Birmingham with the empty stock of a football special from Liverpool. The photograph was taken from the down (Stourbridge line) platform, and the signal box that controlled Handsworth Junction can be seen through the arch of Halfords Lane bridge. The fans had alighted at the up platform on the Wolverhampton line and can be seen making their way from the station through the left arch of the bridge. Albion fans will be interested to know that their team triumphed 3-0 over visiting Everton that day.

The scene today is dominated by the new station, which, unlike its predecessor, is now open every day of the week and provides both main-line services on the Dorridge/Shirley to Worcester axis and frequent Metro services between Wolverhampton St George's and Birmingham Snow Hill, the latter following the route of the old Great Western main line. Halfords Lane bridge can be seen beyond the station as Class 150 DMU No 150002 departs with the 10.56 Great Malvern to Stratford-upon-Avon service on 5 April 2009. *Michael Mensing/JW*

THE HAWTHORNS: The view from Halfords Lane bridge on 15 July 1986 shows Class 31 No 31149 trundling to Handsworth cement terminal along the former down road to Stourbridge with the daily trip service from Bescot. Note the remains of the old platform face in front of the locomotive, which was once the platform for Stourbridge Junction. The up line is still in situ, but heavily overgrown.

The formal opening of the Jewellery Line took place on 24 September 1995 and was an event celebrated along the route with a special train hauled by the Severn Valley Railway's ex-BR Standard

tank No 80079, which stopped off at the major stations for local dignitaries to perform separate opening ceremonies. 'The Black Diamond', as the train was called, reflecting the revived route's association with both the Black Country and the Jewellery Quarter, is seen at The Hawthorns while the opening ceremony for the new station takes place. Scheduled services recommenced on the following day after a gap of 23 years. The station remains incomplete, though, as on the north (left-hand) side construction of the Midland Metro has yet to commence.

The Hawthorns became 'complete' with the north-side extension to accommodate the tram

tracks and platforms for the Midland Metro, which opened in September 1999 and, together with the Jewellery Quarter, became an important interchange point where passengers could change between the two systems to create a host of new journey options. The site required major redevelopment, which included demolition of the old terraced properties on the south side of the site to create space for a substantial car park to enhance the station's park-and-ride credentials. On 5 August 2009 Class 150 No 150014 continues its journey to Kidderminster with the 1409 service from Dorridge.
All JW

SMETHWICK GALTON BRIDGE (HIGH LEVEL): Class 25 No 25057 has just taken the branch from Smethwick Junction, located just beyond the background bridge, with the daily trip to Blue Circle Cement at Handsworth on 19 September 1986. The extension of the line from Stourbridge had a dual advantage, in that it connected with the LNWR at Galton Junction, and by way of an extension from Smethwick Junction, with the Great Western main line at Handsworth Junction. This short spur crossed both the LNWR Stour Valley route (identified by the electrification masts to the right of the train) and the Birmingham Canal by way of a viaduct.

Smethwick Galton Bridge, of all the new stations opened when the Snow Hill to Stourbridge line was reinstated, is perhaps the most exceptional in that it has opened up new travel options by being an interchange with the Birmingham to Wolverhampton Stour Valley route, which is served by the Low Level platforms. The High Level station opened in 1995, and was intended to replace the nearby Smethwick West. The latter actually survived for a further 12 months due to a hitch with the closure procedure. On 5 August 2009 Class 150 No 150014 departs from the High Level platform with the 1526 Kidderminster to Shirley service. *Both JW*

Birmingham Moor Street

BIRMINGHAM MOOR STREET is unquestionably the jewel in the crown of Birmingham's current stations. Unlike its larger and better-known neighbours, it has been renovated and enlarged and offers a totally engaging and traditional atmosphere. It opened on 1 July 1909 and was originally a terminus station positioned at the southern end of the tunnel from Snow Hill station. The North Warwickshire Line had opened 12 months earlier and the station's principal role was to serve the trains of that line as well as to alleviate pressure on Snow Hill. When the route from the south into Snow Hill was severed in March 1967, Leamington Spa line services were diverted into its platforms together with existing North Warwickshire Line trains. The terminus side of the station closed in September 1987 when the new through platforms opened together with the tunnel to the rebuilt Snow Hill. This scene of dereliction dates from the period after 1987 when the terminus side of Moor Street became disused. It is a scene very common to observers of the railway, and is normally a sign that the bulldozers are already waiting to commence their work. However, it was not to be!

Incredibly, this is the present scene at Moor Street, on 20 April 2009. The whole station has been renovated in period Great Western style and is a joy to behold. It is now managed by Chiltern Railways, which, in conjunction with the developers of the nearby multi-million-pound Bull Ring Shopping Centre, has turned the clock back with a vengeance. This is now the booking hall, which took over from the then 'new' 1987 version when the renovation was completed in 2003. *Both GD*

BIRMINGHAM MOOR STREET: Two locally based 2-6-2T 'Prairie' tanks stand at the buffers at Moor Street on 16 July 1955 on recently arrived services. On the left is No 5184 of Leamington Spa, with Tyseley's No 4111 alongside. The locomotives are standing on the traverser table, a feature of Moor Street, and in the background can be seen what looks like the roof of the wagon hoist, which served the basement goods warehouse. A goods warehouse was also built on the west side of the station.

In 2009 we see a near perfect scene at Moor Street – the only thing missing is a train, and for that we will have to wait until 2010 when the terminus platforms will again be brought back into use as part of the ongoing West Midlands resignalling scheme based on the new Saltley Signalling Centre. The brickwork is classic Great Western, and would almost certainly meet the approval of Moor Street architect, GWR 'New Works' engineer Walter Young Armstrong, who was also responsible for rebuilding Snow Hill and the huge fourth span at Paddington. Of particular note is that a water tower has been included in the 2003 renovation in anticipation of Vintage Trains using the terminus for some of its steam services. Another reminder of steam days is the gap beneath the platform, which once accommodated the traverser. *Peter Shoesmith/GD*

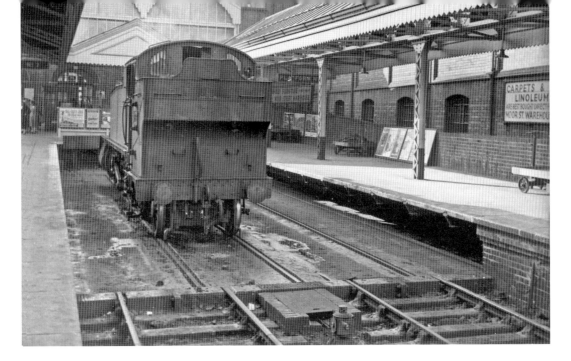

BIRMINGHAM MOOR STREET: In order to maximise the flexibility of the terminus, electrically driven traversers were installed at the buffers in order to release locomotives, instead of the more usual scissors-style crossovers, which took up much-needed platform capacity. The procedure is well illustrated in this scene of 20 April 1957, showing a 'Prairie' tank locomotive standing on the traverser table in the process of being released from its train in order to run round. Each traverser could accommodate anything up to a 'Castle' Class locomotive. To accommodate the lateral movement of the table, a gap was provided beneath the platforms, which can clearly be seen to the right of the locomotive.

The terminus platforms of today have been restored in anticipation of their return to use in 2010 and interestingly the gap provided for the traverse table remains. The present-day scene was recorded on 5 August 2009, and reflects the high standard of the restoration work undertaken at Moor Street. Little change is evident except for the loss of the building on the right-hand platform. *John Dew/GD*

BIRMINGHAM MOOR STREET: For most of its life Moor Street was a terminus station with the main line passing on the east side into Snow Hill Tunnel from which on 12 November 1960 'Castle' No 4085 Berkeley Castle emerges with an up parcels train. Note the wagon hoist on the left, while the parapet and ground ironwork indicates where the Great Western line passes over the LMS line, which at this point is just emerging from New Street South Tunnel. The corner of the distinctive white-stone-clad Marks & Spencer building is just visible beyond the wagon hoist.

On 25 June 2009 Chiltern Railways Class 168 No 168003 calls with the 1212 Snow Hill to London Marylebone service. Note again the period restoration in Great Western style, with the covered footbridge and canopies, which replaced the earlier 'minimalistic' curved corrugated steel construction installed when the through platforms opened in 1987. To the left is the water tower, which has been installed specifically to service steam locomotives, further reinforcing the 'retro' feel of the place. The improvements to the through platforms has been funded by Chiltern Railways alone. *Michael Mensing/GD*

BIRMINGHAM MOOR STREET: Back in 1987, the first phase of the Moor Street redevelopment is under way. The terminus station is still in use and a certain photographer is collecting material for a 'British Railways Past & Present' volume (No 5). The entrance to Snow Hill Tunnel can be seen, and the Rotunda and Marks & Spencer building stand proud against a changing backdrop. Note the redevelopment behind the booking hall, which was an early phase of the reshaping of the Bull Ring area of the city centre.

The full extent of the Moor Street refurbishment, and its key position in the heart of the new vibrant Birmingham city centre, is well illustrated here as Class 150 No 150011 heads for Stratford-upon-Avon with the 0746 service from Kidderminster. Directly above the DMU is the Marks & Spencer building, and to the left the new water tower hides most of the graceful gabled roof of Moor Street's booking hall and concourse. Two Birmingham icons dominate the left-hand side. The Rotunda, a product of the 1960s that was initially unloved but is now very much a 'Brummie' favourite, has recently been extensively refurbished and offers apartments with spectacular city views. In front of it is the equally controversial Selfridges building, a product of the new Bull Ring Shopping Centre. It may be an acquired taste, but is nevertheless now a major landmark and has served to greatly enhance the renaissance of Birmingham in recent years. *Both GD*

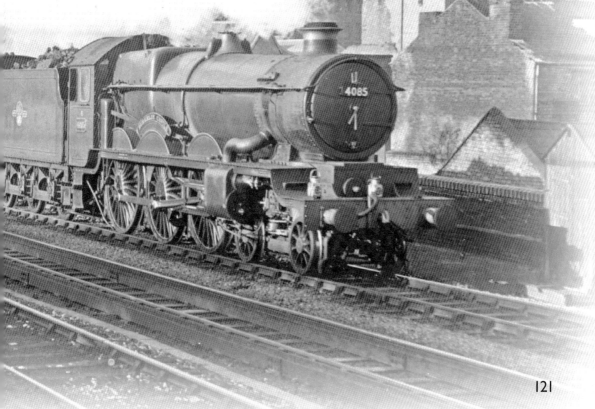

BIRMINGHAM MOOR STREET: It is 20 July 1981 and the Tyseley-based Class 116 DMU has been spruced up in honour of the wedding of HRH Prince Charles and Lady Diana Spencer, which was due to take place in nine days. The DMU is stabled awaiting its next turn, while in the platform is prototype 'Railbus' No 140001, which was undergoing trials on the routes out of Moor Street. The Rotunda stands proud against the city skyline, emblazoned at the top with a 'Coca-Cola' sign, which at the time was the largest neon sign in the UK, and a digital clock, which was equally visible from afar. The car park on the left is where the goods warehouse once stood.

With the Rotunda under renovation, Birmingham's new landmark building, Selfridges' store, now contrasts with the traditional Great Western design of Moor Street. To accommodate the new expanded Bull Ring the area previously occupied by the car park has been taken up by a new roadway, and the old island platform now looks out at Selfridges. Another key development is a significant improvement in the

pedestrian connection with New Street station, the location of which can be pinpointed by the Rotunda. Nowadays it is entirely at road level, whereas previously it was through a warren of underpasses that were not pleasant. Note the rear of ex-Great Western 2-8-0 No 2885, which has been cosmetically restored as is on display at the barrier end of the platform until 2010, when this side of Moor Street will again see train services. For the future, there are plans for a new service from the Camp Hill line stations of Kings Heath and Moseley, which will run into Moor Street via a new chord near Bordesley. *Both GD*

Moor Street to Dorridge

BORDESLEY: No one could criticise the Great Western for ignoring the needs of Birmingham commuters in the southern suburbs. There were no fewer than seven stations in the 6½ miles from Moor Street to Solihull, the first being Bordesley, some three-quarters of a mile from Moor Street. Being on the direct Snow Hill route, it opened in 1855 and probably lost some of its importance with the opening of Moor Street in 1909. On 20 July 1961 '5100' Class 'Prairie' No 5174 crosses from the down relief to the down main line at the head of the 6.25pm Knowle & Dorridge to Birmingham Moor Street commuter train formed of suburban stock. The Camp Hill line, climbing from St Andrew's Junction, can be seen crossing in the background, as

can part of the extensive Bordesley Goods Yard, glimpsed through the right-hand portal of the Camp Hill line overbridge next to the what was the GWR General & Metals Warehouse.

The new bridge carrying the line over Birmingham's middle ring road evidences one of many changes at the south end of Bordesley station. The crossover from the down relief to down main has long been taken out, as has the semaphore signalling. The bridge carrying the Camp Hill line remains, as does the goods warehouse, which is now used as a self-storage facility. Note the new bracket-type signal, which is part of the new West Midlands resignalling scheme that will ultimately reconnect the terminus platforms at nearby Moor Street station. Heading south is Class 150 No 150017 forming the 1634 Worcester Foregate Street to Dorridge service on 27 July 2009. *Michael Mensing/JW*

BORDESLEY was well provided for, despite its proximity to both Snow Hill and Moor Street, with traditional Great Western buildings on both platforms. Look very closely beyond the waiting rooms on the left-hand side (the relief line platform) and there is just a glimpse of the signal box situated at the end of the viaduct that links Bordesley to Moor Street. To the right is a cattle station, the signage for which remains on the retaining wall on the corner of Upper Trinity Street, which runs parallel to the railway at this point. The entrance to the station is at road level beneath the bridge that carries the railway over the busy Coventry Road, the supporting girders of which are just visible at the far end of the platforms. To complete the scene, 'King' No 6020 King Henry IV rushes past with the 5.10pm London Paddington to Wolverhampton Low Level express.

A rather spartan appearance greets the visitor to Bordesley nowadays, reflecting the few trains that actually now call at the station. It gets busy on Saturdays in the football season when Birmingham City are playing, as their ground at St Andrew's is just a short walk away. A couple of breeze-block shelters are the only protection against the elements, and to say that the entrance at street level is less than inviting is perhaps a monumental understatement. The prosperous Birmingham city centre skyline contrasts with the dereliction of the old platform, the remains of which can be seen as Class 150 DMU No 150016 speeds through non-stop with the 16.47 Worcester Foregate Street to Stratford-upon-Avon service on 27 July. *Michael Mensing/JW*

BORDESLEY JUNCTION: A typical pre-1970 inner-city scene is perhaps the best description of the area surrounding Bordesley Junction, with a Stanier 8F 2-8-0 descending the chord from the Camp Hill line (which runs on the embankment behind the locomotive) towards ex-Great Western metals on 4 June 1966. The view is looking towards Bordesley Park Road, Small Heath, from Bolton Road, which is lined with terraced houses that were very much part of any inner-city scene at the time. Note the gap in the left-hand row of houses, which, judging by the state of the brickwork, indicates that the property that once stood there could possibly have been a victim of wartime bombing.

There is a quite different vista from Bolton Road on 8 October 2008. The terraced houses had been demolished by the late 1960s, replaced by a more modern housing estate out of view behind the photographer. Bordesley Park Road is now little more that a stub, truncated out of sight on the other side of the railway, replaced by Bordesley Middleway, part of Birmingham's inner ring road. The old Great Western warehouse, previously hidden behind the terraced houses, is now exposed to view as Freightliner Class 66/5 No 66568 heads south with the 0613 Leeds to Southampton freightliner, which on this day consists of mainly empty wagons. *Peter Shoesmith/GD*

SMALL HEATH is a densely populated area to the south of the city centre, being the third in a string of sizable stations constructed by the Great Western Railway from Snow Hill. It dates back to 1863 and until quite recent times was known as 'Small Heath & Sparkbrook'. Judging by the inquisitive looks from the train crew and platform staff the train is about to depart on a southbound stopping service on 12 April 1962. The locomotive is 'Manor' Class 5MT No 7817 Garsington Manor and the station, of typical Great Western design, consists of two island platforms with the booking hall situated over the tracks at road level. Note the proximity of local housing, which would be a surprise to a visitor at the location today.

The station today is known simply as 'Small Heath' and has lost the platform buildings and canopies that were such a feature. Only the left-hand island platform is now in use by local services running via Snow Hill on the Stourbridge to Dorridge and Shirley axis. The removal of the canopies does reveal the bulk of the booking hall, while on the platform a basic shelter is the only protection against the elements. The area has been redeveloped and the Birmingham inner ring road now runs alongside the railway on the right-hand side, sweeping away the terraced housing that once flanked the station. Rushing through Small Heath on 18 September 2008 is Chiltern Railways Class 168 No 168004 on the 1152 Snow Hill to London Marylebone service. *Peter Shoesmith/GD*

SMALL HEATH: Looking north towards the city from the road bridge that accommodates both Small Heath station's booking hall and Golden Hillock Road on 12 April 1962 reveals a scene of hectic activity. Pulling away from the station past Small Heath signal box is a 4MT 2-6-2T 'Prairie' of the '5100' series with a suburban service, being overtaken by a 'King' Class 4-6-0 at the head of a London Paddington to Wolverhampton express, which will be slowing for its Birmingham Snow Hill stop. Beyond is another 'Prairie' at the head of an up freight, which is taking water; one member of the crew is standing on top of the boiler dealing with the water crane's pipe, while his mate is next to the water crane supervising the process. Small Heath Viaduct, which carries a road across the entire width of the extensive Bordesley Goods Yard, can just be made out in the background.

Look closely at the bottom left-hand corner of the 'present' photograph and you can see the corner of the weighbridge hut, which is in the same position in the earlier picture. Also, there is a glimpse of Small Heath Viaduct between the trees, again on the extreme left. Otherwise there is little else to connect the two scenes, as a Central-liveried three-car Class 150 DMU is led away from Small Heath by a London Midland-liveried Class 153 single-car unit on 29 January 2009. Bordesley Yard still sees traffic, but is now a shadow of its former self following the downturn in the car industry, which was a major customer. The route is still four tracks between Bordesley Junction and Tyseley. *Peter Shoesmith/GD*

TYSELEY is a name that trips easily off the tongue today, due in the main to the nearby locomotive works and museum. However, in historical terms it is a more recent addition to the Great Western's portfolio of inner-Birmingham commuter stations, dating back to 1906. In 1908 the importance of Tyseley increased considerably with the opening of the North Warwickshire Line. This route diverged from the Paddington main line here and ran via Shirley and Stratford-upon-Avon to join the Midland Railway's Birmingham to Bristol main line at Cheltenham Spa, and was important as it broke the Midland's stranglehold on the important Birmingham-Bristol route. On 3 July 1964 'Modified Hall' 5MT 4-6-0 No 7929 Wyke Hall is seen working hard at the head of an up express. Note the traditional goose-neck lamp posts, a feature at the time.

In recent years the station has seen considerable investment, particularly in maintaining its Great Western pedigree, but with upgraded facilities. Indeed, while severely damaged by an arson attack a few years ago, it has been restored to its former glory; after years of closure, the far platforms are now back in use following the recent remodelling of the junction. On 17 October 2008 Network West Midlands-liveried Class 150 DMU No 150010 arrives with the 1055 Stourbridge Junction to Stratford-upon-Avon service. *Peter Shoesmith/GD*

TYSELEY: At the south end of Tyseley, looking from Wharfdale Road bridge, we see brand-new diesel-hydraulic Type 5 (later Class 52) No 1062 Western Courier easing over the junction with an empty stock working on 7 May 1963. The train has crossed over from the main line from Paddington and is about to also cross the North Warwickshire Line tracks in order to gain access to the carriage sidings. On the left a diesel shunter is at the head of a rake of wagons from the goods yard situated on the west side of the running lines. While the Class 52s were all withdrawn from BR service by 1977, a handful have survived, including Western Courier, which is owned by the Western Locomotive Association and has just returned to traffic on the Severn Valley Railway after an extensive overhaul.

The track layout at Tyseley South Junction has for long been a bit of a bottleneck and in 2008 was completely remodelled to allow for higher line speeds for through trains, and an improved layout for both Leamington and Stratford line services. The work is part of a larger resignalling scheme for the West Midlands. On 1 April 2009 Central-liveried Class 150 DMU No 150016 eases towards its booked Tyseley stop with the 0927 Stratford-upon-Avon to Stourbridge Junction service. The distinctive row of terraced properties continues to give the location character. *Michael Mensing/GD*

TYSELEY LOCOMOTIVE DEPOT dates back to 1908, when it replaced a smaller shed at nearby Bordesley. The new depot consisted of two 65-foot turntables linked by a connecting line, and a repair shop on the west of the site. The latter was known as the 'factory' and provided a comprehensive repair service to the shed's allocation of 70-plus locomotives. A combination of tender and tank locomotives formed the core allocation, reflecting the suburban passenger work and freight turns that were the staple work for Tyseley's engines. Three 'Prairie' tanks, probably of the '5100' series, and BR Standard Class 5 No 75020 are seen resting in the 'East' roundhouse on 23 May 1959. Straight ahead is the connecting road running through to the 'West' roundhouse.

The 'East' roundhouse had outlived its 'West' neighbour by five years when it was demolished in 1968, while the 'factory' was closed and demolished in 1964 to make way for a new diesel repair facility, which has now expanded into the current 'Maintrain' Diesel Maintenance & Repair Depot. On 27 August 2009 Class 37 No 37263 is seen undergoing restoration on what was once the connecting road to the 'West' roundhouse. The 'East' turntable survives and sees frequent use turning Tyseley's stable of steam locomotives, while the turntable roads are used for the storage of locomotives and vehicles currently under repair or restoration. Vintage Trains, an offshoot of the Birmingham Railway Museum Trust, provides regular main-line steam-hauled trips, which often commence their journey from their own internal platform, named 'Tyseley Warwick Road'. *Peter Shoesmith/GD courtesy Birmingham Railway Museum*

TYSELEY LOCOMOTIVE DEPOT: The coaling plant and water tower was situated in the body of the yard, which was accessed by two roads descending from an embankment that effectively separated the access lines to each of the roundhouses. This view was taken on 22 November 1964, some two years after a boundary change had transferred responsibility for Tyseley from the Western Region to the London Midland Region. Ex-Great Western 'Manor' No 7805 Broome Manor and recently built BR Standard Class 9F No 92237 provide an interesting comparison of locomotive design as they rest by the coaling stage, which can be seen on the extreme right of the picture. Also, a '4100' series 'Prairie' tank is tucked in at the rear of the 9F. On the left are the carriage sidings, which by this date were being used mainly by the local DMU fleet that was quickly replacing steam, and particularly Tyseley's fleet of 'Prairie' locomotives, on suburban services.

A selection of the current Tyseley fleet reflects the depot's activities on 27 August 2009. On the left is 'Hall' No 4953 Pitchford Hall, awaiting a test run to Stratford-upon-Avon later that day ahead of a couple of main-line duties. Alongside is a classic ex-British Railways 0-6-0 diesel shunter, No 13029 (later renumbered into the D3xxx series). On the right, standing beneath the old coaling plant and water tank, is Class 47 No 47773, one of two Class 47s that now form the backbone of Tyseley's diesel fleet. The new Tyseley Locomotive Works was erected alongside the coaling plant and became operational in 1971 following the acquisition of part of the old depot by the Birmingham Railway Museum Trust in 1969. The site is sandwiched between the DMU stabling point on the left, and the 'Maintrain' Maintenance Depot on the other side of the coaling plant. *Michael Mensing/GD courtesy Birmingham Railway Museum*

ACOCKS GREEN: On 6 July 1959 Stanier 'Black 5' No 45269, heading a down freight, passes beneath the footbridge that links the two platforms at Acocks Green. The station dated back to the opening of the Great Western route north from Oxford via Banbury to Birmingham Snow Hill in 1852, and was known as 'Acocks Green & South Yardley' until the 1960s. It was of typical design with two island platforms accessed via a booking hall at roadway level on the Sherborne Road bridge at the north (city) end of the station.

Only one island platform survives today, as the old suburban platform has now been replaced by a car park for the commuters who now bustle through the station each working day. Accommodation on the surviving platform, which used to serve the fast lines, is minimal and the footbridge has been removed, although the booking hall remains intact. The four-track section of railway that used to run throughout the Birmingham suburban network is now reduced to double-track from Tyseley South Junction and as a consequence pathing is becoming difficult due to the growth in both passenger and freight traffic using the route. On 29 March 2009 Central-liveried Class 150 DMU No 150002 approaches Acocks Green with the 1425 Dorridge to Stourbridge Junction service. *Michael Mensing/GD*

OLTON is a mile south of Acocks Green and 1¾ miles from Solihull, and was typical of the stations on the route, having island platforms serving both the main and relief lines with the characteristic Great Western platform architecture. It was and is very much a commuter station, reflected in this 15 July 1960 view with a Class 116 DMU, representing the new order, standing at the up relief platform, as the old order in the shape of 'King' No 6017 King Edward IV sweeps through on the down main with the 4.10pm London Paddington to Birkenhead express.

The scene at Olton today has, by necessity, to be recorded from the down main platform as the relief line platforms have long since been taken out of use. The disused platform remains in situ, albeit now overgrown, while on the remaining platform the basic structure of the waiting room remains and has even gained a canopy in recent years. The station looks well cared for, and the 'period' lighting and platform floral displays certainly enhance its appearance. On 14 August 2009 Class 153 No 153354 leads an unidentified Class 150 forming the 0928 Dorridge to Stourbridge Junction service. *Michael Mensing/GD*

SOLIHULL was one of the major centres on the Great Western main line through the West Midlands, as this view taken on 5 March 1960 confirms. 'King' No 6001 King Edward VII, heading a down express from London Paddington, has just passed through Solihull station, its volcanic exhaust adding to the murk of the day. It is on the down fast line, with the slow lines to the right. Originally a double-track route, it was quadrupled in 1933. On the left is a sizable goods yard, with an equally well-appointed goods shed.

Of the suburban stations on the route, Solihull probably suffered most from rationalisation in the post-Beeching era, mainly due to its proximity to the newly electrified route from New Street to Euston, which is just a few miles away and was expected to dominate the Birmingham-London axis. With the cut-back to just double track again, Solihull has lost one platform with the now canopy-less accommodation on the remaining platform looking a forlorn sight. In recent years a modern corrugated gable roof has been added. The goods yard was an early casualty, and in the intervening years has seen further redevelopment. Freightliner Class 66/9 No 66955 approaches Streetsbrook Road bridge with the 0858 Southampton to Lawley street Freightliner service. *Peter Shoesmith/GD*

WIDNEY MANOR was not the busiest of the Birmingham suburban stations; It was well provided for, though, as this view taken on 8 July 1959 reveals, with an Inter City DMU charging through forming the 08.10 Birmingham Snow Hill to Carmarthen (via Stratford-upon-Avon) service. The station opened in 1899 and was of a different design from the other stations on the route. A feature of the time, perhaps due to the reduced train service, was that it was always well maintained with flower beds picked out with whitewashed stone and platform ornaments like the windmill, which can be seen just to the left of the DMU.

Rationalisation saw the relief lines, laid in 1933, closed and lifted, leaving the station reduced to little more than 'Halt' status with accommodation comprising only a couple of 'Portakabin'-type shelters. The footbridge, too, was severely cut back and lost both its roof and side panelling. A car park now occupies the land used by the relief lines. On 10 June 1987 a Tyseley-based Class 116 DMU passes with a Birmingham Moor Street to Leamington Spa service.

Widney Manor today is a much busier station. The Birmingham and Solihull conurbation has caught up with and surrounded it, and the station now serves commuters to both Birmingham and London Marylebone. The car park has been expanded and the station boasts a new booking hall and waiting room on the down side, although the facilities on the up side remain more rudimentary. Note that the footbridge has been relocated, and is now at the London end of the station, as well as being of the now standard design. Awaiting departure is Class 150 No 150125 forming the 0845 Stourbridge Junction to Dorridge service. *Michael Mensing/GD (2)*

KNOWLE & DORRIDGE, or just 'Dorridge' as it is now known, is the last station within the Great Western's Birmingham commuter belt and dates back to when the line first opened in 1852. To the south of the station the main line changed from quadruple to double track, while to the north between the station and Bentley Heath level crossing were up and down goods loops. It was from the up goods loop on 15 August 1963 that a 'Pannier' tank locomotive at the head of a rake of car-carriers was signalled in error in front of the 1.00pm up 'Birmingham Pullman' hauled by 'Western' diesel-hydraulic No D1040 Western Queen, then just 11 months old and deputising for a failed 'Blue Pullman' set. Despite an emergency brake application from 80mph, the 'Western' slammed into the rear of the freight at a point corresponding to the southern end of the up platform, causing extensive damage to the locomotive cab and the loss of the driver, co-driver and fireman (as the second man on diesel workings was still referred to at the time). Four years earlier, on 14 August 1959, No 6010 King Charles I slows for signals with the 5.20pm (FO) Wolverhampton Low Level to Paddington service, which, according to the photographer, was at that time more usually in the hands of a 'Grange' or 'Hall', or a 'Castle' on a good day! So for him that day was an even better day!

Dorridge has survived the various economy drives by British Rail reasonably well. The main booking hall remains intact, except for the extreme north end and the loss of its canopy. The waiting room on the island platform remains, albeit with a new corrugated iron roof. The signal box, which was situated at the south end of the island platform (virtually adjacent to the point of impact of the 1963 accident) has long since closed, although Bentley Heath crossing box survived until 2009 when control of the crossing passed to the new West Midlands Signalling Centre at Saltley. Easing out of the up goods loop are Colas Class 47s Nos 47739 Robin of Templecombe and 47727 Rebecca with the 1305 Burton-upon-Trent to Dollands Moor steel empties on 12 March 2009. *Michael Mensing/GD*

KNOWLE & DORRIDGE: In a much earlier scene dating back to the 1930s, before the line was quadrupled, 'Saint' No 2919 Saint Cuthbert, with an up local working, arrives at a station that was to change dramatically within a short time. The buildings are of original Brunel design, but were replaced with structures common to the route when quadrupling took place in 1933.

The station today, albeit much rationalised from that dating back to the quadrupling, still retains original features. The booking hall and passenger facilities on the right have not changed too much, the loss of the original canopy being the most obvious feature. The waiting room on the down side has also been refurbished, and now has a modern version of the Great Western-style canopy that typified this stretch of the line. A London Marylebone service is seen arriving with Class 168 No 168108 forming the 0906 from Kidderminster on 14 August 2009. *Mensing-Osborne collection/GD*

KNOWLE & DORRIDGE is seen again in the pre-quadrupling era in the early 1930s, this time looking towards Birmingham and offering an excellent view of the goods yard on the up side packed with coal wagons. A cattle dock features on the down side, in front of the signal box. The co-acting home signal, necessitated by sighting being obscured by a footbridge beyond the station to the south, gives drivers ample advance warning, while the left-hand arm controls access to the loops beyond the station.

This is the view today from the footbridge at the south end of the station. The goods yard is now the station car park and the relief lines on the left have been rationalised to consist of a station loop, used by terminating local services. The platforms were extended as a consequence of the quadrupling and the signal box was relocated to the extreme south end of the island platform. On 7 August 2009 Class 168 No 168215 departs with the 1512 Birmingham Snow Hill to London Marylebone service. *Mensing-Osborne collection/GD*

North Warwickshire Line: Tyseley to Shirley

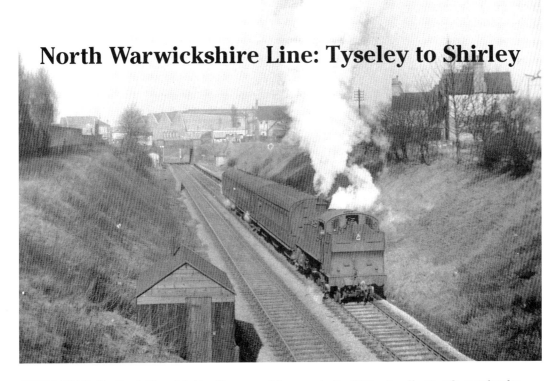

SPRING ROAD: The North Warwickshire Line was a latecomer to the Midlands rail network, opening for passenger trains on 1 July 1908, although freight had been operating since December 1907. It provided a more direct connection to Stratford-upon-Avon, as well as tapping the growing demand for commuter trains from the south Birmingham suburbs. The first of four stations on the route within the Birmingham conurbation was Spring Road Platform, now known simply as Spring Road, a mile from Tyseley and only half a mile from the next station, Hall Green. Only basic amenities were provided from the onset; the booking 'hut', for want of a better word, was in fact a corrugated iron construction, more recently replaced by a 'Portakabin'-type building. On 12 March 1955 a 'Prairie' 2-6-2T draws away with a train bound for Stratford-upon-Avon.

An unsightly car park now straddles the tracks at this point, built for the nearby Lucas Automotive Products factory, which has now been closed. The only point of reference between the two scenes is the ramp of the left-hand (down) platform, just visible beyond Central-liveried Class 150 No 150124 working the 1447 Worcester Shrub Hill to Shirley service on 6 March 2009. *Peter Shoesmith/GD*

HALL GREEN: This tranquil 16 May 1964 scene is enlivened by the window-hanger enjoying the ride behind 'Hall' Class 4-6-0 No 6971 Athelhampton Hall on what is possibly a Snow Hill to Cheltenham Spa semi-fast service. Meanwhile, the young lady sitting outside the waiting room on the Stratford-bound platform seems disinterested with the proceedings. A Birmingham-bound DMU can be seen in the far distance. The station was typical Great Western in design, and opened on the first day of passenger services along the route, 1 July 1908. Also of note is the position of the signal box, the roof of which can be seen above the second and third coaches of the train; this survived until 1984 when control was absorbed by Saltley Panel.

It could be said that Hall Green is one of the great survivors, as except for the loss of the waiting room on the Stratford (up) platform and edging to the footbridge roof it remains structurally intact. Even the metal spiked railings remain, although the signal box was demolished upon closure. The 'preservation' of Hall Green, and other stations on the route, is quite ironic, as 'rationalisation' perhaps did not take place because British Rail went to considerable and, in the opinion of many, underhand efforts to close the line, first in May 1966 which led to a cliff-hanging Court of Appeal decision on 2 May 1969 to prevent BR closing the line from Tyseley to Bearley Junction the next day. BR even had another go in 1985, although this was to cover the 4-mile stretch from Henley in Arden to Bearley Junction. It is good to report that a massive 7,077 objections saw off the threat. So it may well be that 'rationalisation' did not take place because BR expected to demolish the stations instead. On 2 April 2008 Central-liveried Class 150 DMU No 150016 pauses with the 1426 Kidderminster to Shirley service. *Peter Shoesmith/GD*

HALL GREEN: Coal merchants provided the staple trade at most station goods yards, and Hall Green was no exception. The access to the yard from the busy Stratford Road can be seen to the right of the station. The signal box can also be glimpsed on the extreme left, in front of which is the access line to the yard. Note also the spur leading off to the left just in front of the signal box, on the up side. In addition to coal, new Velocette motorcycles were also loaded here, the factory being situated on the right. A BR Derby-built Class 116 DMU, with Driving Motor Brake Second No W50060 leading, heads for Birmingham Moor Street with the 2.05pm service from Shirley on 8 April 1964, as an 0-6-0PT pannier tank locomotive awaits the road with a short rake of mineral wagons.

While the station has changed little, the same cannot be said about the area to the north. The goods yard opened in December 1907, some eight months before the passenger service commenced, and operated through to May 1964. A new prefabricated type of building now occupies the site of part of the motorcycle factory, and the goods yard now provides car parking for the commuters who use the station in ever growing numbers. The two chimneys and the gables of houses in Cateswell Road are the only common denominators between the two scenes. Central-liveried Class 150 No 150015 heads the 1122 Shirley to Worcester Foregate Street service on 24 April 2009. *Michael Mensing/GD*

YARDLEY WOOD: Around 1¼ miles south of Hall Green is the delightful Yardley Wood station (originally known as Yardley Wood Platform), situated in one of the leafier suburbs of Birmingham. The booking hall is situated on Highfield Road, which crosses the railway at this point, and this view is looking down the distinctively fenced pathway to the platforms. Each platform was provided with a solid waiting room and even on 12 March 1955 the area shows little sign of residential development. An 0-6-0PT pannier tank heads a three-coach rake of suburban stock towards Shirley, having deposited a sole city gent who appears to have finished work early, judging by the length of the shadows. For any 'Brummie' the Ansells beer advert will bring back many memories, perhaps some a bit hazier than others! Ansells beer was brewed in the Aston district of Birmingham until 1981.

The arboreal setting continues to dominate the station to the present day, which again shows little change, probably for the same reasons as Hall Green. The two original waiting rooms survive, although that on the Stratford side has been gutted and has lost its canopy. New-style waiting shelters have been provided, but the booking hall and metal spiked railings have survived intact. On 7 April 2009 a Central liveried Class 150 departs with the 1447 Worcester Shrub Hill to Shirley service. *Peter Shoesmith/GD*

SHIRLEY station dates back to the opening of the line to passengers on 1 July 1908, although a goods facility had been in operation since the previous December. It is also the natural termination point for many suburban services, with an hourly service through to Stratford-upon-Avon being the norm for many years. Like the other stations on the line it has miraculously retained most of its buildings and canopies, while the signal box, situated at the north end of the up platform, is one of the last outposts of semaphore signalling in the West Midlands. On 18 June 1979 a Class 116 DMU carrying the short-lived livery of white bodyside with a blue stripe is seen reversing into the holding sidings at the north end of the station. The station goods yard was situated behind the signal box. Note the original Great Western-pattern station nameboard.

The scene today remains much the same, as the station buildings have altered little. New fencing has been erected further back at the rear of the platform. The station signage has been updated, which has resulted in the loss of the attractive ex-GWR nameboard. The signal box and semaphore signalling remain, although they are due to be replaced when the West Midlands resignalling project is fully implemented in 2010. This should bring further benefits to the North Warwickshire Line, as signalling is one of the major constraints for an increased level of services, particularly through to Stratford-upon-Avon. The goods yard, which closed in 1968, is now the car park. On 15 July 2009 Class 150 No 150007 arrives with the 1526 service from Kidderminster. *Both GD*

INDEX OF LOCATIONS